52 WEEK / 3 MINUTE - SPIRITUAL GROWTH JOURNAL – WEEKLY THEMES - DAILY SCRIPTURE

Journal Daily for a Personalized Friendship with God

LEE KOWAL ,MDIV

KINGDOM
LIFE
BOOKS™

COPYRIGHT

Kingdom Life Books_{TM}

52 WEEK / 3 MINUTE SPIRITUAL GROWTH JOURNAL - Weekly Themes - Daily Scripture: Journal Daily for a Personalized Friendship with God

Send inquiries to: Kingdom Life Books, PO Box 4, Lincoln City, Oregon 97367

Print Edition © July 2018 ISBN: 978-1-949261-05-9

Kindle Edition © June 2018 ISBN: 978-1-949261-00-4

ePub Edition © July 2018 ISBN: 978-1-949261-01-1

Hardcover Edition © July 2018 ISBN: 978-1-949261-06-6

Cover Design by *Kingdom Life 365*_{TM}, LLC

*To the praise of the glory of His grace, which He freely bestowed on us in the
Beloved — that the God of our Lord Jesus Christ, the Father of glory, may
give to you a spirit of wisdom and of revelation in the knowledge of Him.*

— EPHESIANS 6:1.17

Thank You PaPa Kowal

CONTENTS

SPIRITUAL GROWTH JOURNAL INTRODUCTION

This journaling devotional relies on God's Word alone to minister & strengthen

The word of God is living and active and sharper than any two-edged sword, and piercing as far as the division of soul and spirit... and able to judge the thoughts and intentions of the heart. Hebrews 4:12 - NAS

~

Scripture alone is allowed to speak for itself — It has the power to change lives!

Weekly spiritual growth themes provide a platform for purposeful meditation and prayer.
Daily focused Bible verses provide 'touch points' between your spirit and His.
A full Year of opportunities for God to draw you by His Love & intimacy!
Challenge yourself to create and personalize your own friendship devotional with God Himself!

Feeding daily on His Word alone will intentionally set your mind toward Him for greater intimacy & strength.

- Time involved is flexible. Make it quick or meditate for longer periods. Use as primary devotional or as quick spiritual uplift.
- Every Week ends with a celebration of prayer, poetry (from sacred hymns), or special quotes to encourage.
- Journaling available in print book.
- Ejournaling place holders available in ebook.
- Sunday's expanded journaling section includes prompts for inspiration.

WHAT IS SPIRITUAL GROWTH?

> 🖼 I am the True Vine, and My Father is the Vinedresser. Abide in Me, and I in you... he who abides in Me, and I in him, bears much fruit; for without Me you can do nothing. John 15: 1,5

THE GOAL - RELATIONSHIP

*C*hristian spiritual growth is deeply rooted in the Person of God Himself.

Lists of personal attributes and accomplishments *may* be outward evidence of spiritual growth, but these do not ultimately define it. Only those attributes and accomplishments flowing from God Himself, living in our heart, are true signs of spiritual growth. Outwardly they may look the same, but inwardly we are spiritually aware of the difference.

> *Living a Christ-centered life filled with peace, joy, and eternal fruit is only possible as we abide with Him in relationship.*

Since spiritual growth and fruit are not possible apart from this vital continuous connection with Him, intentional effort is required. The degree we purposefully pursue this relationship, to know and be known by Him, is directly related to the quality and magnitude of fruit resulting from these pursuits.

> *"Apart from Him you can do nothing."* — *John 15:5*

As we slowly become rooted in Him, we begin to recognize this glorious, *incomprehensible, energizing, life-giving* relationship with God is possible!

LIVING & GROWING ON THE VINE

How to live vitally connected to Him. . .

Spend time in His word daily with intention and desire to seek and know Him. After reading the passage, ask Him to show you the truth, ask questions for understanding — meditate upon His word and your relationship grows. You probably won't hear an audible response, but as you sense His Spirit, you will begin to understand *how* He fills your spirit with joy, contentment, and peace. Then as you come to know Him by His presence, you will also sense His guidance.

As you sense Him lovingly drawing you, you may feel energized and filled with encouragement, strength, and gratitude…This awareness of His presence is only the beginning! As you digest His Word through meditation, your hunger for more of Him will sustain this process in your life!

The practice of the Presence of God — It is the schooling of the soul to find its joy in His Divine Companionship

— BROTHER LAWRENCE, 17TH CENTURY

~

Intentionally and daily:
Feast on His Word
Seek Him purposefully
Learn to recognize His presence

✝✝✝

HOW TO USE THIS DEVOTIONAL

Scripture alone speaks for itself – It has power to change lives

*H*OW IT WORKS —
Weekly spiritual growth themes provide a platform for purposeful meditation and prayer. Daily-focused Bible verses provide touch points between you and God.

As you slowly ponder God's living Word, His Spirit works through it to strengthen your spirit in ways that are unimaginable! As you seek Him earnestly, He provides insight, encouragement, discernment, and reminds us of His continuous presence. Allow your hunger to be satisfied by His energizing life-giving presence!

*B*E INTENTIONAL —
Opportunity for growing spiritually is always at your fingertips, but you will need to make space and time to slow down, get alone, and purposefully engage God & His Word – to invite Him into your daily life and allow this beautiful transfer of communion and growth to occur!

FOUR THINGS TO DO INTENTIONALLY:

1. Go to a quiet place — *Set a time each day to be alone with Him in solitude.*
2. Read the verses slowly and prayerfully — *Prayerfully seek /ask how to apply it to your life.*
3. Ponder and meditate — Spiritual deep dive, ask questions, seek answers: *After each question, stop and let your spirit sense guidance and direction from God's Holy Spirit. Learn to sense His presence.*

4. Journal your journey — *Daily Journaling section with expanded notes on Sundays. Journaling lines available in print book. Ejournaling available in ebook; (✝ ✝ ✝ ✝) icons provide place-holders for five notes.*

(Most devices will allow you to highlight the icon, then click on 'notes' to open device enotes, and color code for convenience. For Sunday's expanded ebook journaling section, store categorized notes at word prompts.)

SUGGESTIONS for JOURNALING

Record meditation questions and answers, prayers, gratitude, conversations with God. Enjoy reading later the notes you take on your spiritual journey.

Sometimes we cannot remember precious thoughts or perceptions from previous devotions. Spiritual growth can occur slowly, and having previous notes for reference or celebration are helpful, encouraging, and needful. The week's insights may also be stored in Sunday's expanded journaling section (both ebook and print book).

❦

*G*row closer in relationship to God by seeking Him through His word.

"For everyone who asks, receives; and he who seeks, finds; and to him who knocks, it will be opened." Luke 11:10 - NAS

❦

PRAYERFULLY SEEK UNDERSTANDING

Asking yourself questions is critical for spiritual understanding —
   Scripture provides a path for your communication with God. Prayerfully ask God to open your eyes to potential adjustments needed to grow closer to Him… He will not withhold truth.
   Review the cadence of your daily activities and interactions with people — take note if you observe how the passage may relate to your personal life (including thought-life), or your understanding of God.

   A question may be, "Since joy is promised from our relationship with God I would like to know what that is like. . . What is it I need to change in order to grow closer to God, and experience His great joy and strength?"

DO I REALLY BELIEVE?

Sometimes the best question is, "Do I really believe this?" —

If you ponder where an unbelief has been buried in 'doing good', it is possible for light to shine in that area and bring growth and strength in Him.

Consider whether there is anything either unseen (spiritual) or seen (unspiritual) that is preventing you from living in full belief of the promises or characteristics of God. Take the steps needed to establish a solid foundation by finding Scripture that will strengthen your faith in that specific area (memorize and meditate upon it).

> *"For the mind set on the flesh is death, but the mind set on the Spirit is life and peace." Romans 8:6 - NAS*

DIG DEEPER

If time permits,

- look up verse reference in Bible and read entire chapter.
- Memorize scripture and take it with you.
- Journal your journey [Daily journaling lines in print version, daily enote place-holders in ebook] & large journaling section every week to capture gratitude, prayers, & conversations with God.

SUBMIT QUICKLY

Quickly submit if you are convicted of any previous misunderstandings of the verse, or if changes are required in your life. Your relationship with God cannot grow if there is unbelief, doubt, worry, or disobedience.

As we submit to & obey Him, He causes our growth. If not, the magnitude of His joy, peace, love, and brilliance of His presence may slip away from your countenance.

Start your journey with a willing & hungry heart! He is always there ready to fill you with His Love.

DON'T GIVE UP!

It is not uncommon for us to commit to following through with a 365 spiritual growth devotional, and then fall behind. Before long we feel so guilty we stop all together.... One thing I have learned over the years, God understands and He is always waiting with open arms!

Please, know that you are not alone. Our enemy Satan would love for you to feel so guilty or discouraged that you stop all together. Do not give in and pray it through!

3rd Millennial life is busy, yet as we grow closer to God we slowly begin to let go of things that no longer bring satisfaction, thus freeing up space for developing a relationship with God. This may not happen over-night.

God never wants you to feel condemned. So be easy on yourself if you are not consistent — Just don't give up!

ULTIMATE GOAL – YOUR RELATIONSHIP WITH HIM TO BE 'ROOTED AND GROUNDED'

See "What is Spiritual Growth?"

"Therefore as you have received Christ Jesus the Lord, so walk in Him, having been firmly rooted and now being built up in Him and established in your faith, just as you were instructed, and overflowing with gratitude." Colossians 2:6-7 - NAS

✝✝✝

OPENING PRAYER

Let the words of my mouth and the meditation of my heart be acceptable in Your sight, O Lord, my Strength and my Redeemer.
Psalms 19:14

O faithful God, thank You for calling me through Your holy Word into the fellowship of Your Son Jesus Christ, my Lord and Savior. I ask for a heart that earnestly seeks you, to know You more personally, to purposefully seek You with passion every morning, and to meditate on Your Word throughout my days —to come to sense Your presence in a tangible way. To feel Your joy, Your peace, Your Love.

Grant that Your Holy Spirit fill my heart and mind with devout desire for truth as I read Your Word and then apply it to the need of my own heart and life. Grant that all my prayers be sincere, rising from a heart that is dedicated to You.

May my words and actions ever reveal that I belong to Jesus, who has purchased me with His own blood. Keep me, I ask You, through Your Holy Spirit from hypocrisy and insincerity, and make my whole being pure and faithful and sincere in every word and act.

I pray You preserve in me a steadfast and unwavering faith in Your Word of truth. Let me be an example to all in love, faith, and purity. Sanctify me wholly, O God of peace, that my whole spirit and soul and body be preserved blameless unto the coming of my Lord and Savior Jesus Christ. Amen.

WEEK 1 – OUR SHEPHERD

Like a shepherd He will tend His flock, In His arm He will gather the lambs, And carry them in His bosom; He will gently lead the nursing ewes. Isaiah 40:11

Monday
I am the good shepherd; and I know My own, and My own know Me, even as the Father knows Me and I know the Father; and I lay down My life for the sheep. John 10:14-15 - NAS

Lord I want to know you! I want you to know me! be my shepheed, guide me, love me, tend to me, keep me on the rightcous path, show me youe ways, LOVE ME! I want to love you as You love me!!

~

Tuesday
But he who enters by the door is a shepherd of the sheep.
To him the doorkeeper opens,
and the sheep hear his voice,
and he calls his own sheep by name,
and leads them out.

When he puts forth all his own, he goes before them,
and the sheep follow him because they know his voice.
And a stranger they simply will not follow,
but will flee from him, because they do not know the voice of strangers.
John 10:2-5 - NAS

―――――――――――――――――――――
―――――――――――――――――――――
―――――――――――――――――――――
―――――――――――――――――――――
―――――――――――――――――――――
―――――――――――――――――――――
―――――――――――――――――――――
―――――――――――――――――――――

❀

Wednesday

As a shepherd looks after his scattered flock when he is with them, so
will I look after my sheep. I will rescue them from all the places where
they were scattered on a day of clouds and darkness. I will bring them
out from the nations and gather them from the countries, and I will
bring them into their own land. Ezekiel 34:12-13 - NKJ

God thank you that we I am never far
from you & from your love!

❀

Thursday

May the God of peace, who through the blood of the eternal covenant
brought back from the dead our Lord Jesus, that great Shepherd of the
sheep, equip you with everything good for doing his will, and may he
work in us what is pleasing to him, through Jesus Christ, to whom be
glory for ever and ever. Amen. Hebrews 13:20-21 - NIV

Thank you Lord, That you have provided
everything I need to do your work &
will! Thank you that you've taken this
babe & raised her up. I will submit to
you & you alone! Continue to do a work
in me, so so that I reflect you!!

_____

_____

_____

_____

Friday
Psalm 23 - AMP
The Lord is my Shepherd
[to feed, to guide and to shield me],
I shall not want.
He lets me lie down in green pastures;
He leads me beside the still and quiet waters.
He refreshes and restores my soul (life);
He leads me in the paths of righteousness for His name's sake.

Even though I walk through the [sunless] valley
of the shadow of death,
I fear no evil, for You are with me;
Your rod [to protect] and Your staff [to guide],
they comfort and console me.

You prepare a table before me
in the presence of my enemies.
You have anointed and refreshed my head with oil;
My cup overflows.
Surely goodness and mercy and unfailing love
shall follow me all the days of my life,
And I shall dwell forever [throughout all my days]
in the house and in the presence of the Lord.

_____

_____

_____

_____

_____

_____

_____

Saturday

JACOB DECLARES THE LORD AS HIS SHEPHERD:

*The God before whom my fathers Abraham and Isaac walked, The God
who has been my shepherd all my life to this day,
The angel who has redeemed me from all evil... Genesis
48:15,16 - NAS*

~

Sunday

*My spirit on your care,
Blest Savior I recline;
You will not leave me to despair,
For You are Love Divine*

*In You I place my trust
On you I calmly rest;
I know You good,
I know You just,
And count Your choice the best*

*Whatever events betide,
Your will they all perform;
Safe in Your breast my head I hide
Nor fear the coming storm.*

*Let good or ill befall,
It must be good for me;
Secure of having You in all,
Of having all in Thee.*

Hymn: My Spirit on Thy Care
Henry F. Lyte, 1834
(Pronouns updated)

~

*J*ournaling **Your Journey** *Spiritual insights - Conversations with God - Favorite verses - Prayers - Struggles, Joys...*

_____
_____
_____
_____
_____
_____
_____
_____
_____
_____
_____
_____
_____
_____
_____
_____

This Week's Gratitude - Praise - Thanksgiving

_____
_____
_____
_____
_____
_____
_____
_____
_____
_____
_____
_____
_____
_____
_____

✝✝✝

WEEK 2 - LOVE IS

[God Is Love] Beloved, let us love one another, for love is from God; and everyone who loves is born of God and knows God. 1 John 4:7

Monday

LOVE IS THE GREATEST COMMANDMENT: *"Teacher, which is the greatest commandment in the Law?" Jesus replied: "'Love the Lord your God with all your heart and with all your soul and with all your mind. This is the first and greatest commandment. And the second is like it: Love your neighbor as yourself." Matthew 22:36-38 - NIV*

_____
_____
_____
_____
_____
_____
_____
_____

∽

Tuesday

LOVE IS SPIRITUAL FRUIT: *"Sow for yourselves righteousness, reap the fruit of unfailing love." Hosea 10:12 - NIV*

LOVE IS ABSENCE OF FEAR: *"There is no fear in love, but perfect love casts out fear. For fear has to do with punishment, and whoever fears has not been perfected in love." 1 John 4:18 - ESV*

_____
_____
_____
_____
_____
_____
_____
_____

~

Wednesday

LOVE IS ABIDING IN GOD: *"And we have come to know and have believed the love which God has for us. God is love, and the one who abides in love abides in God, and God abides in him."*
1 John 4:16 - NAS

_____
_____
_____
_____
_____
_____
_____

~

Thursday

YOUR LOVE IS SET UPON WHAT YOU TREASURE:
Do not lay up for yourselves treasures upon earth, where moth and rust destroy, and where thieves break in and steal. But lay up for yourselves treasures in heaven, where neither moth nor rust destroys, and where thieves do not break in or steal; for where your treasure is, there will your heart be also. Matthew 6:19-21 - NAS

_____
_____
_____
_____
_____
_____
_____

Friday

Love endures with patience and serenity,
love is kind and thoughtful, and is not jealous or envious;
love does not brag and is not proud or arrogant.

It is not rude; it is not self-seeking, it is not provoked
[nor overly sensitive and easily angered];
it does not take into account a wrong endured.

It does not rejoice at injustice,
but rejoices with the truth [when right and truth prevail].

Love bears all things [regardless of what comes],
believes all things [looking for the best in each one],
hopes all things [remaining steadfast during difficult times],
endures all things [without weakening].

Love never fails [it never fades nor ends].
1 Corinthians 13:4-8 - AMP

∼

Saturday

For now [in this time of imperfection] we see in a mirror dimly
[a blurred reflection, a riddle, an enigma], but then
[when the time of perfection comes we will see reality] face to face.

Now I know in part [just in fragments],
but then I will know fully, just as I have been fully known [by God].

And now there remain: faith [abiding trust in God and His promises],
hope [confident expectation of eternal salvation],
love [unselfish love for others growing out of God's love for me],
these three [the choicest graces]; but the greatest of these is love.
1 Corinthians 13:12-13 - AMP

_____
_____
_____
_____
_____
_____
_____

~

Sunday

LOVE IS OUR NEED:

"The single desire that dominated my search for delight was simply to love and to be loved."

— AUGUSTINE OF HIPPO

Prayer

Heavenly Father, I come in Jesus name with a heart full of gratitude that You have guided me safely to this point in my life, and have opened my eyes to begin seeking Your love in a fresh new way. I ask that You take me by the hand and guide my feet into the paths of Your righteousness so that I may reflect Your love to those around me. Help me to become evermore aware of Your glorious presence moment by moment, and grow closer to You day by day in vital relationship. Give me the strength to resist more earnestly the allurements of sin and anything that causes me to stray from the fullness of Your glorious friendship. In Jesus Name. Amen

~

*J**ournaling Your Journey** Spiritual insights - Conversations with God - Favorite verses - Prayers - Struggles, Joys...*

_____
_____
_____
_____
_____
_____
_____
_____
_____
_____

_____
_____
_____
_____
_____
_____
_____

This Week's Gratitude - Praise - Thanksgiving

_____
_____
_____
_____
_____
_____
_____
_____
_____
_____
_____
_____
_____
_____
_____
_____
_____

✝✝✝

WEEK 3 - WISDOM

The mouth of the righteous utters wisdom, And his tongue speaks justice. Psalm 37:30

Monday
The fear of the LORD is the beginning of wisdom; all who follow his precepts have good understanding. To him belongs eternal praise. So teach us to number our days, That we may present to Thee a heart of wisdom. Psalms 111:10;90:12 - NAS

_____

_____

_____

_____

_____

_____

_____

∾

Tuesday
Who among you is wise and intelligent?
Let him by his good conduct show his [good] deeds with the gentleness and humility of true wisdom. But if you have bitter jealousy and selfish ambition in your hearts, do not be arrogant, and [as a result] be in defiance of the truth.

This [superficial] wisdom is not that which comes down from above, but is earthly (secular), natural (unspiritual), even demonic. For where jealousy and selfish ambition exist, there is disorder [unrest, rebellion] and every evil thing and morally degrading practice.

But the wisdom from above is first pure [morally and spiritually undefiled], then peace-loving [courteous, considerate], gentle, reasonable [and willing to listen], full of compassion and good fruits. It is unwavering, without [self-righteous] hypocrisy [and self-serving guile].

And the seed whose fruit is righteousness (spiritual maturity) is sown in peace by those who make peace [by actively encouraging goodwill between individuals]. James 3:13-18 - AMP

⁓

Wednesday
I guide you in the way of wisdom and lead you along straight paths. For I will give you words and wisdom that none of your adversaries will be able to resist or contradict. Proverbs 4:11; Luke 21:15 - NIV

⁓

Thursday
Oh, the depth of the riches of the wisdom and knowledge of God! How unsearchable his judgments, and his paths beyond tracing out! Romans 11:33 - NIV

_____
_____
_____
_____
_____
_____
_____
_____

~

Friday

Therefore everyone who hears these words of Mine, and acts upon them, may be compared to a wise man, who built his house upon the rock. And the rain descended, and the floods came, and the winds blew, and burst against that house; and yet it did not fall, for it had been founded upon the rock. Matthew 7:24-25 - NAS

_____
_____
_____
_____
_____
_____
_____
_____

~

Saturday

The wise in heart will be called understanding, and sweetness of speech increases persuasiveness. Understanding is a fountain of life to one who has it, but the discipline of fools is folly. The heart of the wise instructs his mouth and adds persuasiveness to his lips. Pleasant words are a honeycomb, sweet to the soul and healing to the bones.
Proverbs 16:21-24 - NAS

_____
_____
_____
_____
_____
_____
_____
_____

Sunday

Prayer
Heavenly Father, I earnestly request that You fill me...
with the knowledge of His will in all spiritual wisdom
[with insight into His purposes],
and in understanding [of spiritual things],
so that you will walk in a manner worthy of the Lord
[displaying admirable character,
moral courage, and personal integrity],

to [fully] please Him in all things, bearing fruit
in every good work and steadily growing
in the knowledge of God
[with deeper faith, clearer insight and fervent love for His precepts];

[I pray that I may be] strengthened and invigorated
with all power, according to His glorious might,
to attain every kind of endurance and patience with joy;
giving thanks to the Father, who has qualified us to share
in the inheritance of the saints (God's people) in the Light.

Based on Colossians 1:9-12 - AMP

~

*J**ournaling Your Journey** Spiritual insights - Conversations*
with God - Favorite verses - Prayers - Struggles, Joys...

_____

_____

_____

_____

_____

_____

_____

_____

_____

_____

_____

_____

_____

_____

_____

_____

_____

_____

This Week's Gratitude - Praise - Thanksgiving

✝✝✝

WEEK 4 – FRUIT OF THE MOUTH I

Fruit from the Vine is eternal – Without Him you can do nothing
John 15

Monday
The mouth of the righteous man utters wisdom, and his tongue speaks what is just. The law of his God is in his heart; his feet do not slip.
Psalm 37:30, 31 - NIV

~

Tuesday
The mouth speaks out of that which fills the heart -
A soothing tongue is a tree of life, But perversion in it crushes the spirit.
Matthew 12:34; Proverbs 15:4 - NAS

~

Wednesday
*For with the heart man believes, resulting in righteousness, and with
the mouth he confesses, resulting in salvation. Romans 10:10 - NAS*

~

Thursday
Death and life are in the power of the tongue. Proverbs 18:21 - KJV

~

Friday
*We cannot but speak the things which we have seen and heard.
Acts 4:20 - KJV*

Saturday

Everyone therefore who shall confess Me before men, I will also confess him before My Father who is in heaven. Matthew 10:32 - NAS

～

Sunday

*Oh for a thousand tongues to sing
My great Redeemer's praise,
The glories of my God and King,
The triumphs of His grace!*

*My gracious Master and my God,
Assist me to proclaim,
To spread thro' all the earth abroad,
The honors of Your name*

Charles Wesley, 1739

(Pronouns Updated)

～

J **ournaling Your Journey** *Spiritual insights - Conversations with God - Favorite verses - Prayers - Struggles, Joys...*

This Week's Gratitude - Praise - Thanksgiving

✝✝✝

WEEK 5 – FRUIT OF THE MOUTH II

Good Roots Produce Good Fruit

Monday

Do not let any unwholesome talk come out of your mouths, but only what is helpful for building others up according to their needs, that it may benefit those who listen. And do not grieve the Holy Spirit of God, with whom you were sealed for the day of redemption.

Get rid of all bitterness, . . . Be kind and compassionate to one another, forgiving each other, just as in Christ God forgave you.
Ephesians 4:29-32 - NIV

~

Tuesday

The tongue of the righteous is as choice silver, ... The lips of the righteous feed many.
Proverbs 10:20,21 - NAS

The tongue of the wise is health. Proverbs 12:18 - KJV

_____
_____
_____
_____
_____
_____
_____
_____

~

Wednesday
Let your speech at all times be gracious and pleasant, seasoned with salt, so that you will know how to answer each one [who questions you]. Colossians 4:6 - AMP

_____
_____
_____
_____
_____
_____
_____
_____

~

Thursday
Like apples of gold in settings of silver Is a word spoken in right circumstances. Like an earring of gold and an ornament of fine gold Is a wise reprover to a listening ear. Proverbs 25:11,12 - NAS

_____
_____
_____
_____
_____
_____
_____
_____

Friday
*The wise in heart will be called understanding, and sweet speech
increases persuasiveness and learning [in both speaker and listener].
Understanding (spiritual insight) is a [refreshing and boundless]
wellspring of life to those who have it, but to give instruction and
correction to fools is foolishness.*

*The heart of the wise instructs his mouth [in wisdom] and adds
persuasiveness to his lips. Pleasant words are like a honeycomb, sweet
and delightful to the soul and healing to the body.*
Proverbs 16:21-24 - AMP

∽

Saturday
*Then those who feared the LORD spoke to one another,
and the LORD gave attention and heard it,
and a book of remembrance was written before Him for those who fear
the LORD and who esteem His name. Malachi 3:16 - NAS*

∽

Sunday
*Take my voice and let me sing
Always, only, for my King;
Take my lips and let them be
Filled with messages from You (Thee).*

Take my will and make it Yours (Thine)
It shall be no longer mine;
Take my heart, it is Your own,
It shall be Your royal throne

Frances R. Havergal, 1874

(Pronouns Updated)

∽

*J*ournaling Your Journey *Spiritual insights - Conversations*
with God - Favorite verses - Prayers - Struggles, Joys...

_____
_____
_____
_____
_____
_____
_____
_____
_____
_____
_____
_____
_____
_____
_____
_____

This Week's Gratitude - Praise - Thanksgiving

_____
_____
_____
_____
_____
_____
_____
_____
_____
_____
_____
_____
_____

✠✠✠

WEEK 6 – PRECIOUS NAME OF JESUS

Behold the Lamb of God! John 1:36

Monday

And His name will be called Wonderful, Counselor, Mighty God, Everlasting Father, Prince of Peace. — … and His name is called The Word of God. And on His robe and on His thigh He has a name written, "KING OF KINGS, AND LORD OF LORDS."
Isaiah 9:6; Revelation 19:13,16 - NKJ

_____

_____

_____

_____

_____

_____

_____

_____

~

Tuesday

Your name is like perfume poured out. - Therefore, to you who believe, He is precious. Song of Songs 1:3; 1 Peter 2:7 - NKJ

_____
_____
_____
_____
_____
_____
_____
_____

≈

Wednesday

Therefore God exalted Him to the highest place and gave Him the name that is above every name, that at the name of Jesus every knee should bow, ... every tongue acknowledge that Jesus Christ is Lord, to the glory of God the Father. Philippians 2:9, 10, 11 - NIV

_____
_____
_____
_____
_____
_____
_____
_____

≈

Thursday

He is clothed with a robe dipped in blood, and His name is called The Word of God. — In His days Judah will be saved, And Israel will dwell securely; And this is His name by which He will be called, 'The Lord our righteousness.' —Therefore the Lord Himself will give you a sign: Behold, a virgin will be with child and bear a son, and she will call His name Immanuel.
Revelation 19:13; Jeremiah 23:6; Isaiah 7:14 - NAS

_____
_____
_____
_____
_____
_____
_____
_____

Friday

...you were not redeemed with perishable things like silver or gold from your futile way of life inherited from your forefathers, but with precious blood, as of a lamb unblemished and spotless, the blood of Christ. 1 peter 1:18,19 - NAS

~

Saturday

So this is what the Sovereign LORD says: "See, I lay a stone in Zion, a tested stone, a precious cornerstone for a sure foundation; the one who relies on it will never be stricken with panic. — Now to you who believe, this stone is precious. But to those who do not believe, "The stone the builders rejected has become the capstone,"
Isaiah 28:16; 2 Peter 2:7 - NIV

~

Sunday

How sweet the name of Jesus sounds
in a believer's ear!
It soothes our sorrows, heals our wounds,
and drives away our fear.

It makes the wounded spirit whole
and calms the troubled breast; '
tis manna to the hungry soul,

and to the weary, rest.

O Jesus, shepherd, guardian, friend,
my Prophet, Priest, and King,
my Lord, my Life, my Way, my End,
accept the praise I bring.

John Newton, 1779

~

ournaling Your Journey Spiritual insights - Conversations
with God - Favorite verses - Prayers - Struggles, Joys...

_____
_____
_____
_____
_____
_____
_____
_____
_____
_____
_____
_____
_____
_____
_____

This Week's Gratitude - Praise - Thanksgiving

_____
_____
_____
_____
_____
_____
_____
_____
_____
_____
_____
_____

WEEK 7 - SPIRITUAL SIGHT

Do not be wise in your own eyes. Proverbs 3:7

Monday
The lamp of the body is the eye; if therefore your eye is clear, your whole body will be full of light. But if your eye is bad, your whole body will be full of darkness. If therefore the light that is in you is darkness, how great is the darkness! Matthew 6:22-23 - NAS

_____
_____
_____
_____
_____
_____
_____
_____

∽

Tuesday
But the one who hates his brother is in the darkness and walks in the darkness, and does not know where he is going because the darkness has blinded his eyes. 1 John 2:11 - ESV

_____
_____
_____
_____
_____

_____
_____
_____
_____

~

Wednesday

*And even if our gospel is veiled, it is veiled to those who are perishing,
in whose case the god of this world has blinded the minds of the
unbelieving, that they might not see the light of the gospel of the glory
of Christ, who is the image of God.*
2 Corinthians 4:3-4 - NAS

_____
_____
_____
_____
_____
_____
_____
_____

~

Thursday

*The LORD said to Moses, "Make a snake and put it up on a pole;
anyone who is bitten can look at it and live."*

*Just as Moses lifted up the snake in the desert, so the Son of Man must
be lifted up, that everyone who believes in him may have eternal life.*
Numbers 21:8; John 3:14-15 - NIV

_____
_____
_____
_____
_____
_____
_____
_____

Friday

So we fix our eyes not on what is seen,
but on what is unseen.
For what is seen is temporary,
but what is unseen is eternal.
2 Corinthians 4:18 - NIV

_____
_____
_____
_____
_____
_____
_____
_____
_____

∽

Saturday

Be sober, be watchful. Your adversary the devil, prowls around like a
roaring lion, seeking whom he may devour. 1 Pet. 5:8 - ESV

_____
_____
_____
_____
_____
_____
_____
_____

∽

Sunday

The Two Listeners

To see Me you must bring Me your cares and show Me your heart of
Trust. Then as you leave your cares you become conscience of My
presence... The eye of the soul is the will. A single eye to God's glory.
Seek in all things His kingdom first. You do not need to see far ahead.
Just one step at a time.

When you are told to seek first the Kingdom of God, the first step is to
secure that your will is for that Kingdom. A single eye to God's glory.
Desiring nothing less than that His Kingdom come. Seeking in all
things the advance of His Kingdom. Know no values but Spiritual

values. No profit but that of Spiritual gain. Seek in all things His Kingdom first. Only seek material gain when that gain will mean a gain for My Kingdom. Get away from money values altogether. Walk with Me. Learn of Me. Talk to Me. Here lies your true happiness.

~

*J*ournaling Your Journey *Spiritual insights - Conversations with God - Favorite verses - Prayers - Struggles, Joys...*

_____
_____
_____
_____
_____
_____
_____
_____
_____
_____
_____
_____
_____
_____
_____
_____
_____
_____

This Week's Gratitude - Praise - Thanksgiving

_____
_____
_____
_____
_____
_____
_____
_____
_____
_____
_____
_____
_____
_____
_____
_____
_____

✝✝✝

WEEK 8 – PEACE I

Peace is a way of life, His name is Jesus

Monday

Peace I leave with you; My peace I give to you; not as the world gives, do I give to you. Let not your heart be troubled, nor let it be fearful. John 14:27 - NAS

_____
_____
_____
_____
_____
_____
_____
_____

∼

Tuesday
For God is not a God of confusion but of peace. 1 Corinthians 14:33 - NAS

_____
_____
_____
_____
_____
_____
_____
_____

Wednesday

Do not be anxious about anything, but in everything, by prayer and petition, with thanksgiving, present your requests to God. And the peace of God, which transcends all understanding, will guard your hearts and your minds in Christ Jesus. Philippians 4:6-7 - NIV

⁓

Thursday

For thus the Lord God, the Holy One of Israel, has said, "In repentance and rest you shall be saved, In quietness and trust is your strength." - In peace I will lie down and sleep, for you alone, Lord, make me dwell in safety. Isaiah 30:15; Psalm 4:8 - NAS

⁓

Friday

Blessed are the peacemakers, for they shall be called sons of God. - Great peace have those who love your law, and nothing can make them stumble. *Matthew 5:9; Psalm 119:165 - NAS*

Saturday

For the mind set on the flesh is death, but the mind set on the Spirit is life and peace. Romans 8:6 - NAS

∾

Sunday

Lord, make me an instrument of your peace. Where there is hatred, let me sow love; Where there is injury, pardon; Where there is doubt, faith; Where there is despair, hope; Where there is darkness, light; Where there is sadness, joy.

O Divine Master, grant that we may not so much seek to be consoled as to console; Not so much to be understood as to understand; Not so much to be loved as to love. For it is in giving that we receive, it is in pardoning that we are pardoned, it is in dying that we are born to eternal life.

— ATTRIBUTED TO FRANCIS OF ASSISI

∾

J **ournaling Your Journey** *Spiritual insights - Conversations with God - Favorite verses - Prayers - Struggles, Joys...*

This Week's Gratitude - Praise - Thanksgiving

✝✝✝

WEEK 9 – PEACE II

Those who walk in Him have unexplainable peace

Monday
But now in Christ Jesus you who once were far away have been brought near through the blood of Christ. For he himself is our peace.
Ephesians 2:13-14 NIV

~

Tuesday
Finally, believers, whatever is true, whatever is honorable and worthy of respect, whatever is right and confirmed by God's word, whatever is pure and wholesome, whatever is lovely and brings peace, whatever is admirable and of good repute; if there is any excellence, if there is anything worthy of praise, think continually on these things [center your mind on them, and implant them in your heart].

The things which you have learned and received and heard and seen in me, practice these things [in daily life], and the God [who is the

*source] of peace and well-being will be with you. Philippians
4:8-9 - AMP*

_____

_____

_____

_____

_____

_____

_____

_____

≈

Wednesday

*Now may the Lord of peace Himself continually grant you peace in every
circumstance. - peace from Him who is and who was and who is to come.
2 Thessalonians 3:16; Revelations1:4 - NAS*

_____

_____

_____

_____

_____

_____

_____

_____

≈

Thursday

RENEW YOUR SPIRITUAL VITALITY FOR PEACE:

*Now no chastening seems to be joyful for the present, but painful; nevertheless,
afterward it yields the peaceable fruit of righteousness to those who have been
trained by it. Therefore strengthen the hands which hang down, and the feeble
knees, and make straight paths for your feet, so that what is lame may not be
dislocated, but rather be healed. Pursue peace with all people, and holiness,
without which no one will see the Lord. Hebrews 12:11-14 - NKJ*

_____

_____

_____

_____

_____

_____

_____

<u>Friday</u>
But the wisdom from above is first pure [morally and spiritually undefiled], then peace-loving [courteous, considerate], gentle, reasonable [and willing to listen], full of compassion and good fruits.

It is unwavering, without [self-righteous] hypocrisy [and self-serving guile]. And the seed whose fruit is righteousness (spiritual maturity) is sown in peace by those who make peace [by actively encouraging goodwill between individuals]. James 3:17-18 - AMP

_____
_____
_____
_____
_____
_____
_____
_____

≈

<u>Saturday</u>
Aaronic Blessing
The LORD bless you, and keep you; The LORD make His face shine on you, And be gracious to you; The LORD lift up His countenance on you, And give you peace. Numbers 6:24-26 - NKJ

_____
_____
_____
_____
_____
_____
_____

≈

<u>Sunday</u>

When peace like a river attendeth my way, when sorrows like sea billows roll; whatever my lot, thou hast taught me to say, "It is well, it is well with my soul."

Though Satan should buffet, though trials should come,

let this blest assurance control:
that Christ has regarded my helpless estate,
and has shed his own blood for my soul.

Horatio Gates Spafford, 1873

~

J **ournaling Your Journey** *Spiritual insights - Conversations*
with God - Favorite verses - Prayers - Struggles, Joys...

_____
_____
_____
_____
_____
_____
_____
_____
_____
_____
_____
_____
_____
_____
_____
_____
_____

This Week's Gratitude - Praise - Thanksgiving

_____
_____
_____
_____
_____
_____
_____
_____
_____
_____
_____
_____
_____

✝✝✝

WEEK 10 - JOY OF JESUS

The closer we abide in Him the deeper our joy – And do not be grieved, for the joy of the Lord is your strength, Nehemiah 8:10

Monday
"I am the true vine...Abide in Me and I in you... These things I have spoken to you, that My joy may remain in you, and that that your joy may be full." John 15:1,4,11 - KJV

_____

_____

_____

_____

_____

_____

_____

~

Tuesday
As the Father has loved me, so have I loved you. Abide in my love. If you keep my commandments, you will abide in my love, just as I have kept my Father's commandments and abide in his love. These things I have spoken to you, that my joy may be in you, and that your joy may be full. This is my commandment, that you love one another as I have loved you. John 15:9 -12 - ESV

_____

_____

_____

_____
_____
_____
_____
_____

∾

Wednesday

*I pray for them... I will remain in the world no longer, but they are
still in the world,... Holy Father, protect them by the power of your
name--... so that they may be one as we are one... I am coming to you
now, but I say these things while I am still in the world, so that they
may have the full measure of my joy within them.*
John 17:9,11,13 - NIV

_____
_____
_____
_____
_____
_____
_____

∾

Thursday

*Therefore, since we are surrounded by so great a cloud of witnesses, let
us also lay aside every weight, and sin which clings so closely, and let us
run with endurance the race that is set before us,*

*looking to Jesus, the founder and perfecter of our faith, who for the joy
that was set before him endured the cross, despising the shame, and is
seated at the right hand of the throne of God.*
Hebrews 12:1-2 - ESV

_____
_____
_____
_____
_____
_____
_____

Friday

*The Lord your God is in your midst, a mighty one who will save; he
will rejoice over you with gladness; he will quiet you by his love; he will
exult over you with loud singing. Zephaniah 3:17 - ESV*

≈

Saturday

*Thus says the Lord: "In this place ..., there shall be heard again the
voice of mirth and the voice of gladness, the voice of the bridegroom
and the voice of the bride, the voices of those who sing, as they bring
thank offerings to the house of the Lord: 'Give thanks to the Lord of
hosts, for the Lord is good, for his steadfast love endures forever!'"
Jeremiah 33:10-11 - ESV*

≈

Sunday

*O Holy Spirit, enter in
And in our hearts Your work begin,
Your temple sure to make us;
Sun of the soul, Your Light Divine,
Around and in us brightly shine,
To joy and gladness wake us
That we, in You truly living,
To You giving prayer unceasing,
May in love be still increasing*

O gentle Dew, from heaven now fall
With power upon the hearts of all,
Your tender love instilling,
That heart to heart more closely bound,
In kindly deeds be fruitful found,
The law of love fulfilling,
Dwell thus in us; Envy banish;
Strife will vanish where You live.
Peace and love and joy You gives us.

Michael Schirmer, 1640

(Pronouns updated)

∾

*J*ournaling *Your Journey* Spiritual insights - Conversations
with God - Favorite verses - Prayers - Struggles, Joys...

_____
_____
_____
_____
_____
_____
_____
_____
_____
_____
_____
_____
_____
_____
_____
_____
_____

This Week's Gratitude - Praise - Thanksgiving

_____
_____
_____
_____
_____
_____
_____
_____
_____

✝✝✝

WEEK 11 - HUMILITY

Submission to God's peace & rest – "I dwell in the high and holy place, with him who has a contrite and humble heart..." Isaiah 57:15

Monday
Take My yoke upon you, and learn from Me,
for I am gentle and humble in heart;
and you shall find rest for your souls.
For My yoke is easy, and My load is light.
Matthew 11:29-30 - NIV

_____

_____
_____
_____
_____
_____
_____
_____
_____
_____

∾

Tuesday

Heaven is My throne and earth is My footstool. —
For My hand made all these things,
Thus all these things came into being,
declares the LORD.
But to this one I will look,
To him who is humble and contrite of spirit,
and who trembles at My word.
Isaiah 66:2 - NAS

_____

_____

_____

_____

_____

_____

_____

_____

~

Wednesday

Humble yourselves, therefore, under the mighty hand of God, that He may
exalt you at the proper time, casting all your anxiety upon Him, because He
cares for you. 1 Peter 5:6-7 - NAS

_____

_____

_____

_____

_____

_____

_____

~

Thursday

But the humble will inherit the land, And will delight themselves in abundant
prosperity. Psalm 37:11 - NAS

_____

_____

_____

_____

_____

_____
_____
_____

∼

Friday
Blessed are the poor in spirit, for theirs is the kingdom of heaven. . . Blessed
are the meek, for they shall inherit the earth.
Matthew 5: 3,5 - ESV

_____
_____
_____
_____
_____
_____
_____

∼

Saturday
Humble yourselves before the Lord, and he will lift you up.
James 4:10 - NIV

_____
_____
_____
_____
_____
_____
_____

∼

Sunday
These are a few ways we can practice Humility:

- *To speak as little as possible of one's self*
- *To mind one's own business*
- *Not to want to manage other people's affairs*
- *To avoid curiosity*
- *To accept contradictions and corrections cheerfully*
- *To pass over the mistakes of others*

- *To accept being slighted, forgotten, and disliked*
- *To be kind and gentle even under provocation*
- *Never to stand on one's dignity*
- *To Choose always the hardest*

Mother Teresa

~

*J*ournaling **Your Journey** *Spiritual insights - Conversations with God - Favorite verses - Prayers - Struggles, Joys...*

_____
_____
_____
_____
_____
_____
_____
_____
_____
_____
_____
_____
_____
_____
_____

This Week's Gratitude - Praise - Thanksgiving

_____
_____
_____
_____
_____
_____
_____
_____
_____
_____
_____
_____
_____
_____

WEEK 12 – LOVE OF GOD

His Love for Us is Unmeasurable

Monday

*"For God so [greatly] loved and dearly prized the world,
that He [even] gave His [One and] only begotten Son,
so that whoever believes and trusts in Him [as Savior]
shall not perish, but have eternal life.*

*For God did not send the Son into the world to judge
and condemn the world [that is,
to initiate the final judgment of the world],
but that the world might be saved through Him.*
John 3:16-17 - AMP

_____

_____

_____

_____

_____

_____

_____

~

Tuesday

But when the goodness and loving kindness of God our Savior appeared,
He saved us, not because of works done by us in righteousness,
but according to his own mercy, by the washing of regeneration
and renewal of the Holy Spirit, whom he poured out on us richly
through Jesus Christ our Savior, so that being justified by his grace
we might become heirs according to the hope of eternal life.
Titus 3:4-7 - ESV

_____
_____
_____
_____
_____
_____
_____
_____

~

Wednesday

Such hope [in God's promises] never disappoints us,
because God's love has been abundantly poured out within our
hearts through the Holy Spirit who was given to us.
While we were still helpless [powerless to provide for our salvation],
at the right time Christ died [as a substitute] for the ungodly.

Now it is an extraordinary thing for one to willingly give his life
even for an upright man, though perhaps for a good man
[one who is noble and selfless and worthy]
someone might even dare to die.

But God clearly shows and proves His own love for us,
by the fact that while we were still sinners, Christ died for us.
Roman 5:5-8 - AMP

_____
_____
_____
_____
_____
_____
_____
_____

Thursday

But because of his great love for us, God, who is rich in mercy, made us alive with Christ even when we were dead in transgressions-it is by grace you have been saved. And God raised us up with Christ and seated us with him in the heavenly realms in Christ Jesus. Ephesians 2:4-6- NIV

Friday

Neither height nor depth, nor anything else in all creation, will be able to separate us from the love of God that is in Christ Jesus our Lord. Romans 8:39 - NIV

Saturday

See how great a love the Father has bestowed upon us, that we should be called children of God; and such we are. 1 John 3:1 - NAS

~

Sunday

Prayer of Apostle Paul:

For this reason, I bow my knees before the Father, from whom every family in heaven and on earth derives its name, that He would grant you, according to the riches of His glory, to be strengthened with power through His Spirit in the inner man; so that Christ may dwell in your hearts through faith; and that you, being rooted and grounded in love, may be able to comprehend with all the saints what is the breadth and length and height and depth, and to know the love of Christ which surpasses knowledge, that you may be filled up to all the fulness of God.

Now to Him who is able to do exceeding abundantly beyond all that we ask or think, according to the power that works within us, to Him be the glory in the church and in Christ Jesus to all generations forever and ever. Amen.
Ephesians 3:14-21 - NAS

~

*J*ournaling Your Journey *Spiritual insights - Conversations with God - Favorite verses - Prayers - Struggles, Joys...*

_____
_____
_____
_____
_____
_____
_____
_____
_____
_____
_____
_____
_____
_____
_____
_____

This Week's Gratitude - Praise - Thanksgiving

_____
_____
_____
_____

_____
_____
_____
_____
_____
_____
_____
_____
_____
_____
_____
_____

✝✝✝

WEEK 13 – THE HOLY SPIRIT

Our Personal Comforter & Guide

Monday

But the Helper, the Holy Spirit, whom the Father will send in My name, He will teach you all things, and bring to your remembrance all things that I said to you. John 14:26 - NIV

_____
_____
_____
_____
_____
_____
_____
_____

∾

Tuesday

But when He, the Spirit of truth, comes, He will guide you into all the truth; for He will not speak on His own initiative, but whatever He hears, He will speak; and He will disclose to you what is to come. He shall glorify Me; for He shall take of Mine, and shall disclose it to you. John 16:13, 14 - NAS

_____
_____
_____
_____

_____
_____
_____

∼

Wednesday
And in that day you will ask Me no question. Truly, truly, I say to you,
if you shall ask the Father for anything, He will give it to you in My
name. Until now you have asked for nothing in My name; ask, and you
will receive, that your joy may be made full.
John 16:23, 24 - NAS

_____
_____
_____
_____
_____
_____
_____

∼

Thursday
If you then, though you are evil, know how to give good gifts to your
children, how much more will your Father in heaven give the Holy
Spirit to those who ask Him*!*
Luke 11:13 - NIV

You have not, because you ask not.
James 4:2 - NKJ

_____
_____
_____
_____
_____
_____
_____

∼

Friday

Jesus answered her, "If you knew the gift of God and who it is that asks you for a drink, you would have asked him and he would have given you living water." John 4:10 - NIV

∾

Saturday

Moreover, I will give you a new heart and put a new spirit within you; and I will remove the heart of stone from your flesh and give you a heart of flesh. Ezekiel 36:26 - NAS

∾

Sunday

Come, Holy Spirit, Creator blest,
Vouchsafe within our souls to rest;
Come with Your grace an heavenly aid
And fill the hearts which You have made.

To You, the Comforter we cry,
To You, the Gift of God Most High,
The Fount of life, the Fire of love,
The soul's Anointing from above.

Rhabanus Maurus, 856

~

*J*ournaling Your Journey *Spiritual insights - Conversations with God - Favorite verses - Prayers - Struggles, Joys...*

_____
_____
_____
_____
_____
_____
_____
_____
_____
_____
_____
_____
_____
_____
_____
_____
_____
_____
_____

This Week's Gratitude - Praise - Thanksgiving

_____
_____
_____
_____
_____
_____
_____
_____
_____
_____
_____
_____
_____
_____
_____

✝✝✝

WEEK 14 – PUT ON...

Put on Love, Humility, Kindness – Put on Jesus

Monday
Put ... on the Lord Jesus Christ.... put on a heart of compassion, kindness, humility, gentleness and patience; bearing with one another, and forgiving each other, whoever has a complaint against anyone; just as the Lord forgave you, so also should you. And beyond all these things put on love, which is the perfect bond of unity.
Romans 13:14; Colossians 3:12-14 - NAS

_____

_____
_____
_____
_____
_____
_____
_____
_____
_____

∾

Tuesday

For this perishable must put on the imperishable,
and this mortal must put on immortality.
But when this perishable will have put on the imperishable,
and this mortal will have put on immortality,
then will come about the saying that is written,
"Death is swallowed up in victory."
1 Corinthians 15:53-54 - NAS

_____
_____
_____
_____
_____
_____
_____
_____
_____

≈

Wednesday

Let us therefore lay aside the deeds of darkness and put on the armor of light. .
. put on the Lord Jesus Christ, and make no provision for the flesh in regard to
its lusts. And put on the new self, which in the likeness of God has been created
in righteousness and holiness of the truth.
Romans 13:12,14; Ephesians 4:24- NAS

_____
_____
_____
_____
_____
_____
_____
_____
_____

≈

Thursday

Put on the full armor of God,
that you may be able to stand firm against the schemes of the devil -
put on the breastplate of faith and love, and as a helmet, the hope of
salvation. Ephesians 6:11; 1 Thessalonians 5:8 - NAS

_____
_____
_____
_____
_____
_____
_____
_____

∽

Friday
I put on righteousness, and it clothed me;
My justice was like a robe and a turban.
I was eyes to the blind, And feet to the lame.
I was a father to the needy.
Job 29:14-16 - NIV

_____
_____
_____
_____
_____
_____
_____
_____

∽

Saturday
Awake, awake, Clothe yourself in your strength,
O Zion; Clothe yourself in your beautiful garments,
O Jerusalem, the holy city. Clothe yourselves with humility toward one
another, for God is opposed to the proud, but gives grace to the humble.
Isaiah 52:11; Peter 5:5 - NAS

_____
_____
_____
_____
_____
_____
_____
_____

∽

Sunday
The Two Listeners

Health — Peace — Joy — Patience — Endurance, they all come from contact with Me. Oh! It is the glorious way, the upward way, the wonderful discoveries, the tender intimacies, the amazing, almost incomprehensible, understanding. Truly the christian life will change all disappointment, even if only momentary, into Joy. Change each complaint into laughter. — Life with Me — is a Love story. Leave all to Me. Trust in Me.

~

Journaling Your Journey Spiritual insights - Conversations with God - Favorite verses - Prayers - Struggles, Joys...

_____
_____
_____
_____
_____
_____
_____
_____
_____
_____
_____
_____
_____
_____
_____
_____

This Week's Gratitude - Praise - Thanksgiving

_____
_____
_____
_____
_____
_____
_____
_____
_____
_____
_____

WEEK 15 - WALKING

His footsteps - Our Pathway – Palm 85:13

Monday
Again Jesus spoke to them, saying, "I am the light of the world, whoever follows Me will not walk in the darkness, but shall have the light of life."…
John 8:12 - ESV

Walk in love, as Christ loved us, and gave Himself up for us, a fragrant offering and sacrifice to God. Ephesians 5:2 - ESV

≈

Tuesday
All things become visible when they are exposed by the light, for everything that becomes visible is light. Therefore it says, "Awake, sleeper, And arise from the dead, And Christ will shine on you." look carefully then how you walk, not as unwise men, but as wise, making the best of your time, because the days are evil.
Ephesians 5:13-16 - ESV

_____
_____
_____
_____
_____
_____
_____
_____
_____

≈

Wednesday
For we know that if the earthly tent which is our house is torn down,
we have a building from God, a house not made with hands,
eternal in the heavens. Therefore, being always of good courage,
and knowing that while we are at home in the body
we are absent from the Lord-- for we walk by faith, not by sight.
2 Corinthians 5:2,6-7 - NAS

_____
_____
_____
_____
_____
_____
_____
_____

≈

Thursday
Walk by the Spirit, and you will not gratify the desires of the flesh. For the
desires of the flesh are against the Spirit, and the desires of the Spirit are
against the flesh, for these are opposed to each other...
Galatians 5:16-17 - ESV

_____
_____
_____
_____
_____
_____
_____
_____

≈

Friday

*How blessed is the man who does not walk in the counsel of the wicked,
Nor stand in the path of sinners, Nor sit in the seat of scoffers!
But his delight is in the law of the LORD, And in His law he meditates day
and night. And he will be like a tree firmly planted by streams of water,
Which yields its fruit in its season, And its leaf does not wither;
And in whatever he does, he prospers. Psalm 1:1-3 - NAS*

∼

Saturday

*Therefore we have been buried with Him through baptism into death,
in order that as Christ was raised from the dead through the glory of the
Father, so we too might walk in newness of life. — As you therefore have
received Christ Jesus the Lord, so walk in Him, having been firmly rooted
and now being built up in Him and established in your faith,
just as you were instructed, and overflowing with gratitude.
Romans 6:4; Colossians 2:6-7 - NAS*

∼

Sunday

*Oh, that the Lord would guide my ways
To keep His statutes still!
Oh, that my God would grant me grace
To know and do His will*

Order my foot-steps by thy word

And make my heart sincere;
Let sin have no dominion, Lord,
But keep my conscience clear.

Isaac Watts, 1719

~

*J*ournaling *Your Journey* Spiritual insights - Conversations with God -
Favorite verses - Prayers - Struggles, Joys...

_____
_____
_____
_____
_____
_____
_____
_____
_____
_____
_____
_____
_____
_____
_____

This Week's Gratitude - Praise - Thanksgiving

_____
_____
_____
_____
_____
_____
_____
_____
_____
_____
_____
_____
_____

WEEK 16 – JESUS OUR REDEEMER

God was manifest in the flesh. – The kindness and love of God our Savior toward man appeared. 1 Timothy 3:16; Titus 3:4

Monday

There is one God, and one mediator between God and men, the man Christ Jesus. 1 Timothy 2:5 - KJV

We have one who speaks to the Father in our defense-- Jesus Christ, the Righteous One. 1 John 2:1 - NIV

Turn to me and be saved, all you ends of the earth; for I am God, and there is no other. Isaiah 45:22 - NIV

_____
_____
_____
_____
_____
_____
_____
_____

～

Tuesday

Since the children have flesh and blood, he too shared in their humanity so that by his death he might destroy him who holds the power of death-- that is, the devil-- and free those who all their lives were held in slavery by their fear of death. Hebrews 2:14 - NIV

_____
_____
_____
_____
_____
_____
_____
_____

~

Wednesday

But now in Christ Jesus you who once were far away have been brought near through the blood of Christ. For he himself is our peace.
Ephesians 2:13, 14 - NIV

_____
_____
_____
_____
_____
_____
_____
_____

~

Thursday

By his own blood he entered in once into the holy place, having obtained eternal redemption for us. And for this cause he is the mediator of the new testament, that by means of death, for the redemption of the transgressions that were under the first testament, they which are called might receive the promise of eternal inheritance.
Hebrews 9:12, 15 - KJV

_____
_____
_____
_____
_____
_____
_____
_____

~

Friday

Surely our griefs He Himself bore,
And our sorrows He carried;
Yet we ourselves esteemed Him stricken,
Smitten of God, and afflicted.

But He was pierced through for our transgressions,
He was crushed for our iniquities;
The chastening for our well-being fell upon Him,
And by His scourging we are healed. Isaiah 53:4-5 - NAS

~

Saturday

Behold, My Servant, whom I uphold;
My chosen one *in whom* My soul delights.
I have put My Spirit upon Him;
He will bring forth justice to the nations.

He will not cry out or raise *His voice,*
Nor make His voice heard in the street.
A bruised reed He will not break
And a dimly burning wick He will not extinguish;
He will faithfully bring forth justice.

I am the Lord, I have called You in righteousness,
I will also hold You by the hand and watch over You,
And I will appoint You as a covenant to the people,
As a light to the nations,
To open blind eyes,
To bring out prisoners from the dungeon
And those who dwell in darkness from the prison.
Isaiah 42:1-2,6-7 - NAS

_____
_____
_____
_____
_____

≈

Sunday

Prayer

Lord Jesus, risen gloriously from the dead, I worship You as my living Savior, who redeemed me to be Your own eternally; and I adore You as conqueror of satan, sin, and death. Joy fills my heart as I worship You, the eternal, living Lord; for death cannot hold us in terror, and even the grave cannot keep our dust and ashes. I need not weep despairing tears; for You will raise me and all believers to eternal life. Take full possession of my heart today. Cleanse me, keep me, let not the cares and worries of life rob me of the joy of Your Gospel! Yours be the praise, throughout all eternity. Amen. Hallelujah! Amen.

≈

*J*ournaling Your Journey *Spiritual insights - Conversations with God - Favorite verses - Prayers - Struggles, Joys...*

_____
_____
_____
_____
_____
_____
_____
_____
_____
_____
_____
_____
_____
_____

This Week's Gratitude - Praise - Thanksgiving

_____
_____
_____

✝✝✝

WEEK 17 – EATING/DRINKING I

Our spirit requires food and water for strength and growth just as our body requires nourishment

Monday
Yet He commanded the clouds above,
And opened the doors of heaven;
And He rained down manna upon them to eat,
And gave them food from heaven.
Man did eat the bread of angels;
He sent them food in abundance.
Psalm 78:23-25 - NAS

Tuesday

I am the living bread that came down out of heaven;
if anyone eats of this bread, he shall live forever;
and the bread also which I shall give
for the life of the world is My flesh.
John 6:51 - NAS

~

Wednesday

Jesus said to them, "My food is to do the will of Him who sent Me, and to
accomplish His work." John 4:34 - NIV

~

Thursday

Blessed are those who hunger and thirst for righteousness, for they shall be
satisfied. Matthew 5:6 - NAS

Friday

In that day, A vineyard of wine, sing of it! I, the LORD, am its keeper; I water it every moment. Lest anyone damage it, I guard it night and day.
Isaiah 27:2-3 - NAS

_____

_____

_____

_____

_____

_____

_____

_____

~

Saturday

Does not the ear test words, As the palate tastes its food? - I will meditate on Thy precepts, And regard Thy ways. I shall delight in Thy statutes; I shall not forget Thy word.
Job 12:11; Psalm 119:15-16 NAS

_____

_____

_____

_____

_____

_____

_____

~

Sunday

Special C. Spurgeon Devotional

I will meditate in thy precepts. Psalm 119:15 - KJV

There are times when solitude is better than society, and silence is wiser than speech. We should be better Christians if we were more alone, waiting upon God, and gathering through meditation on his Word spiritual strength for labor in his service.

We ought to muse upon the things of God, because we get the real nutrition out of them. Truth is something like the cluster of the vine: if we would have wine from it, we must bruise it; we must press and squeeze it many times. The bruiser's feet must come down joyfully upon the bunches, or else the juice will not flow; and they must well tread the grapes, or else much of the precious liquid will be wasted. So we must, by meditation, tread the clusters of truth, if we would get the wine of consolation from it.

Likewise, our bodies are not supported by merely taking food into the mouth, but the process which really supplies the muscle, and the nerve, and the sinew, and the bone, is the process of digestion. It is by digestion that the outward food becomes assimilated with the inner life.

Our souls are not nourished merely by listening awhile to this, and then to that, and then to the other part of divine truth. Hearing, reading, marking, and learning, all require inwardly digesting to complete their usefulness, and the inward digesting of the truth lies for the most part in meditating upon it.

Why is it that some Christians, although they hear many sermons, make but slow advances in the divine life? Because they neglect their closets, and do not thoughtfully meditate on God's Word. They love the wheat, but they do not grind it; they would have the corn, but they will not go forth into the fields to gather it; the fruit hangs upon the tree, but they will not pluck it; the water flows at their feet, but they will not stoop to drink it.

From such folly deliver us, O Lord, and be this our resolve this morning, "I will meditate in thy precepts."

∽

*J*ournaling *Your Journey* Spiritual insights - Conversations with God - Favorite verses - Prayers - Struggles, Joys...

_____
_____
_____
_____
_____
_____
_____
_____
_____
_____
_____
_____
_____
_____
_____
_____

This Week's Gratitude - Praise - Thanksgiving

✝✝✝

WEEK 18 - EATING/DRINKING II

He is Our Spirit's Food and Water

Monday

I am the bread of life. . . This is the bread which comes down out of heaven, so that one may eat of it and not die. For My flesh is true food, and My blood is true drink. . . He who eats My flesh and drinks My blood abides in Me, and I in him. John 6:48,50,55-56 - NAS

~

Tuesday

They drink their fill of the abundance of Thy house; And Thou dost give them to drink of the river of Thy delights. For with Thee is the fountain of life; In Thy light we see light. Psalm 36:8-9 - NAS

_____

_____

_____

~

Wednesday
Whoever drinks of the water that I shall give him shall never thirst;
but the water that I shall give him shall become in him a well of water
springing up to eternal life. John 4:14 - NAS

_____

_____

_____

_____

_____

_____

~

Thursday
My son, eat honey, for it is good,
Yes, the honey from the comb is sweet to your taste;
Know that wisdom is thus for your soul;
If you find it, then there will be a future,
And your hope will not be cut off.
Proverbs 24:13-14 - NAS

_____

_____

_____

_____

_____

_____

_____

~

Friday
Drinking bad water

Has a nation ever changed its gods? (Yet they are not gods at all.) But my people have exchanged their Glory for worthless idols. Be appalled at this, O heavens, and shudder with great horror," declares the LORD. My people have committed two sins: They have forsaken me, the spring of living water, and have dug their own cisterns, broken cisterns that cannot hold water. Jeremiah 2:11-13 - NIV

≈

Saturday

Ho! Every one who thirsts, come to the waters; And you who have no money come, buy and eat. Come, buy wine and milk Without money and without cost. Why do you spend money for what is not bread, And your wages for what does not satisfy? Listen carefully to Me, and eat what is good, And delight yourself in abundance.
Isaiah 55:1-2 - NAS

≈

Sunday
Oh, well for me that, strengthened -
With heavenly food and comfort here,
Howe'er my course be lengthened,
I now may serve You free from fear!
Away, then, earthly pleasure!
All earthly gifts are vain;
I seek a heavenly treasure -

My home I long to gain,
My God, where I shall praise You -
Where none my peace destroy,
And where my soul shall raise You -
Glad songs in endless joy."

Johann Rist, 1651
(Pronouns updated)

~

ournaling Your Journey Spiritual insights - Conversations with God -
Favorite verses - Prayers - Struggles, Joys...

_____
_____
_____
_____
_____
_____
_____
_____
_____
_____
_____
_____
_____
_____
_____
_____

This Week's Gratitude - Praise - Thanksgiving

_____
_____
_____
_____
_____
_____
_____
_____
_____
_____
_____
_____
_____

WEEK 19 – LIGHT IN DARKNESS

I have come as Light into the world, so that everyone who believes
in Me will not remain in darkness. John 12:46

Monday
*When I sit in darkness the Lord will be a light unto me. In the
multitude of my anxieties within me, Your comforts delight my soul.
Micah 7:8; Psalm 94:19 - NKJ*

_____

_____

_____

_____

_____

_____

_____

_____

~

Tuesday
*When you pass through the waters, I will be with you;
And through the rivers, they will not overflow you.
When you walk through the fire, you will not be scorched,
Nor will the flame burn you. For I am the LORD your God,
The Holy One of Israel, your Savior
Isaiah 43:2, 3 - NAS*

_____

_____

_____

~

Wednesday
*Even though I walk through the valley of the shadow
of death, I fear no evil; for Thou art with me;
Thy rod and Thy staff, they comfort me.
Psalm 23:4 - NAS*

~

Thursday
*The LORD is my light and my salvation;
whom shall I fear? the LORD is the strength of my life;
of whom shall I be afraid? Psalm 27:1 - KJV*

~

Friday
*I will lead the blind by ways they have not known, along unfamiliar
paths I will guide them; I will turn the darkness into light before them
and make the rough places smooth. These are the things I will do; I will
not forsake them. Isaiah 42:16 - NIV*

_____
_____
_____
_____
_____
_____
_____
_____

≈

Saturday

When I am afraid, I will put my trust in Thee. In God, whose word I praise, In God I have put my trust; I shall not be afraid. What can mere man do to me? Psalms 56:3, 4 - NAS

_____
_____
_____
_____
_____
_____
_____
_____

≈

Sunday

Prayer

Heavenly Father, I am so very thankful to have You as the light in my life. You are my light, my hope, my rock in the storm. You are my hiding place — I have no other refuge in an hour of darkness. Gracious Lord, give me strength to carry on when troubles come. Remove worries and anxious fears and give me grace to trust in You who is my loving Father. Thank You for all blessings. I place my confidence in You and Your eternal Love. In Jesus Name I pray. Amen.

*J*ournaling **Your Journey** *Spiritual insights - Conversations with God - Favorite verses - Prayers - Struggles, Joys...*

_____
_____
_____

This Week's Gratitude - Praise - Thanksgiving

✝✝✝

WEEK 20 - OUR CROSS

Our Cross is Our Peace & Rest

Monday
If anyone wishes to come after Me,
let him deny himself, and take up his cross daily,
and follow Me. Luke 9:23 - NAS

~

Tuesday
...that if One died for all, then all died;
and He died for all, that those who live should live
no longer for themselves, but for Him who died for them
and rose again.
2 Corinthians 5:14, 15 - NKJ

~

Wednesday
*Or don't you know that all of us who were baptized
into Christ Jesus were baptized into his death?
We were therefore buried with him through baptism
into death in order that, just as Christ was
raised from the dead through the glory of the Father,
we too may live a new life. Romans 6:3-4 - NIV*

~

Thursday
*If then you have been raised up with Christ,
keep seeking the things above, where Christ is,
seated at the right hand of God. Set your mind on the things above,
not on the things that are on earth. For you have died
and your life is hidden with Christ in God.
Colossians 3:1-3 - NAS*

Friday

*For those who live according to the flesh set their minds
on the things of the flesh, but those who live according to the Spirit,
the things of the Spirit. For to be carnally minded is death,
but to be spiritually minded is life and peace.*
Romans 8:5-6 - NKJ

_____
_____
_____
_____
_____
_____
_____
_____

❧

Saturday

*If you are insulted because of the name of Christ, you are blessed, for the
Spirit of glory and of God rests on you. If you suffer, it should not be as a
murderer or thief or any other kind of criminal, or even as a meddler.
However, if you suffer as a Christian, do not be ashamed, but praise God that
you bear that name.* 1 Pet. 4:14-16 - NIV

_____
_____
_____
_____
_____
_____
_____
_____

❧

Sunday

The Two Listeners
If I yet pleased men, I should not be the servant of Christ.
Galatians 1:10 - KJV

*Self dethroned – that is the lesson, . . . For each blow to the life of self you must
at the same time embrace and hold fast the new Life with Me. . . Ever seek to
set aside the valuation of the world, judge only according to the values of*

Heaven. Delight in My Love. Try to live in the rapture of the kingdom. Joy in Me.

~

*J*ournaling Your Journey *Spiritual insights - Conversations with God - Favorite verses - Prayers - Struggles, Joys...*

_____

_____
_____
_____
_____
_____
_____
_____
_____
_____
_____
_____
_____
_____
_____
_____
_____

This Week's Gratitude - Praise - Thanksgiving

_____
_____
_____
_____
_____
_____
_____
_____
_____
_____
_____
_____
_____
_____

✝✝✝

WEEK 21 - SPIRIT WARFARE

Spiritual FIGHT for Spiritual PEACE

Monday

Away with you, Satan! For it is written,
'You shall worship the LORD your God,
and Him only you shall serve.'
Then the devil left Him,
and behold, angels came and ministered to Him.
- Resist the devil, and he will flee from you.
Matthew 4:10, James 4:7 - NKJ

_____

_____

_____

_____

_____

_____

_____

_____

_____

≈

Tuesday

For our struggle is not against flesh and blood [contending only with
physical opponents], but against the rulers, against the powers, against
the world forces of this [present] darkness, against the spiritual forces
of wickedness in the heavenly (supernatural) places.
Ephesians 6:12 - AMP

_____
_____
_____
_____
_____
_____
_____
_____
_____

~

Wednesday

Put on the full armor of God [for His precepts are like the splendid armor of a heavily-armed soldier], so that you may be able to [successfully] stand up against all the schemes and the strategies and the deceits of the devil...

Therefore, put on the complete armor of God, so that you will be able to [successfully] resist and stand your ground in the evil day [of danger], and having done everything [that the crisis demands], to stand firm [in your place, fully prepared, immovable, victorious].

So stand firm and hold your ground, having tightened the wide band of truth (personal integrity, moral courage) around your waist and having put on the breastplate of righteousness (an upright heart), and having strapped on your feet the gospel of peace in preparation [to face the enemy with firm-footed stability and the readiness produced by the good news].

Above all, lift up the [protective] shield of faith with which you can extinguish all the flaming arrows of the evil one. And take the helmet of salvation, and the sword of the Spirit, which is the Word of God.
Ephesians 6:11,13-17 - AMP

_____
_____
_____
_____
_____
_____
_____
_____

~

Thursday

To fear the LORD is to hate evil. - Have nothing to do with the fruitless deeds of darkness, but rather expose them. - Don't you know that a little yeast works through the whole batch of dough?
Proverbs 8:13; Ephesians 5:11; 1 Corinthians 5:6 - NIV

~

Friday

Be sober [well balanced and self-disciplined], be alert and cautious at all times. That enemy of yours, the devil, prowls around like a roaring lion [fiercely hungry], seeking someone to devour. But resist him, be firm in your faith [against his attack—rooted, established, immovable], knowing that the same experiences of suffering are being experienced by your brothers and sisters throughout the world. [You do not suffer alone.] . . 1 Pet. 5:8-9 - AMP

~

Saturday

"You will not surely die," the serpent said to the woman.(Eve) -- But I am afraid that just as Eve was deceived by the serpent's cunning, your minds may somehow be led astray from your sincere and pure devotion to Christ. Genesis 3:4; 2 Corinthians 11:3 - NIV

~

Sunday

The Two Listeners
Lord, give us Power to conquer temptation as Thou didst in the wilderness.

The very first step towards conquering temptation is to see it as temptation. To dissociate yourself from it. Not to think of it as something resulting from your tiredness, or illness, or poverty, when you feel you might well excuse yourself for yielding, but first to realize very fully that when you have heard My voice and are going to fulfill your mission to work for Me and to draw souls to Me, you must expect a mighty onslaught from the evil one, who will endeavor with all his might to frustrate you, and to prevent your good work. Expect that. Then when these little temptations, or big ones come, you will recognize them as planned by evil to thwart Me. Then for very love of Me you will conquer.

— "AND LEAD ME NOT INTO TEMPTATION, BUT
DELIVER ME FROM EVIL: FOR THINE IS THE
KINGDOM, AND THE POWER, AND THE GLORY,
FOR EVER." MATTHEW 6:13 - KJV

~

*J*ournaling **Your Journey** *Spiritual insights - Conversations with God - Favorite verses - Prayers - Struggles, Joys...*

_____
_____
_____
_____

This Week's Gratitude - Praise - Thanksgiving

_____
_____
_____
_____
_____
_____
_____
_____
_____
_____
_____
_____
_____
_____

✝✝✝

WEEK 22 - COMMUNING WITH GOD

Key to Spiritual Growth & Fruit

Monday

O God, you are my God; earnestly I seek you;
My soul thirsts for you; my flesh faints for you,
As in a dry and weary land where there is no water.
When I remember you upon my bed,
And meditate on you in the watches of the night;
For you have been my help,
And in the shadow of your wings I will sing for joy.
My soul clings to you; your right hand upholds me.
Psalm 63:1;6-8 - ESV

Tuesday

Abide in Me, and I in you. As the branch cannot bear fruit of itself, unless it abides in the vine, so neither can you, unless you abide in Me. I am the vine, you are the branches; he who abides in Me, and I in him, he bears much fruit; for apart from Me you can do nothing. John 15:4-5 - NAS

∽

Wednesday

Here I am! I stand at the door and knock. If anyone hears my voice and opens the door, I will come in and eat with him, and he with me.
Revelation 3:20 - NIV

∽

Thursday

Jesus prayer for all believers: *That they may all be one; even as Thou, Father, art in Me, and I in Thee, that they also may be in Us.*
John 17:21 - NAS

Friday
One thing I have desired of the LORD, That will I seek: That I may dwell in the house of the LORD All the days of my life, To behold the beauty of the LORD, And to inquire in His temple. Psalm 27:4 - NAS

_____
_____
_____
_____
_____
_____
_____
_____

∾

Saturday
Jesus our example:
Very early in the morning, while it was still dark, Jesus got up, left the house and went off to a solitary place, where he prayed. Mark 1:35 - NIV

_____
_____
_____
_____
_____
_____
_____

∾

Sunday

Prayer
Heavenly Father, with praise and joy I look up to You as the Helper and Deliverer who has heard my prayers. Fasten my heart and hope in You, and let my strivings and desire be directed to the treasures of Your love. As long as I am in the land of my pilgrimage, hold my hand; and increase my awareness of Your glorious presence keeping me every moment. Help me to make space and time to spend with You daily, so that our relationship may grow in strength and love. In the name of Jesus Christ my Lord. Amen

∾

*J*ournaling **Your Journey** *Spiritual insights - Conversations with God - Favorite verses - Prayers - Struggles, Joys...*

_____
_____
_____
_____
_____
_____
_____
_____
_____
_____
_____
_____
_____
_____
_____
_____
_____
_____
_____

This Week's Gratitude - Praise - Thanksgiving

_____
_____
_____
_____
_____
_____
_____
_____
_____
_____
_____
_____
_____
_____
_____
_____
_____

✝✝✝

WEEK 23 – OUR CONFIDENCE

Our Confidence is Found Resting in His Strength – Isaiah 30:15

Monday
But he who listens to me shall live securely,
And shall be at ease from the dread of evil. Proverbs 1:33 - NAS

_____
_____
_____
_____
_____
_____
_____
_____

∼

Tuesday
But Jesus immediately said to them: "Take courage! It is I. Don't be afraid." -
Your life is hidden with Christ in God. Matthew 14:27; Colossians 3:3 - NIV

_____
_____
_____
_____
_____
_____
_____
_____

Wednesday

He who dwells in the shelter of the Most High will rest in the shadow of the Almighty. He will cover you with his feathers, and under his wings you will find refuge; his faithfulness will be your shield and rampart. You will not fear the terror of night, nor the arrow that flies by day, Psalms 91:1,4-5 - NIV

~

Thursday

God is our refuge and strength, a very present help in trouble. Therefore will not we fear. - LORD, thou hast been our dwelling place in all generations. Psalms 46:1, 2 - KJV

~

Friday

...for whoever touches you touches the apple of his eye-- Zechariah 2:8 - NIV

Saturday

Fear ye not, stand still, and see the salvation of the LORD. The LORD shall fight for you, and ye shall hold your peace. - My presence shall go with thee, and I will give thee rest. Exodus 14:13, 14; 33:14 - KJV

_____

_____

_____

_____

_____

_____

_____

_____

~

Sunday

The Two Listeners

Have no fear. A very beautiful future lies before you. Let it be a new life, a new existence, in which in every single moment you are conscious of Me. Just say, "Jesus conquers" – "Jesus saves" – in the face of every doubt, every fear. Take more time to be alone with Me. Sense My presence, My touch is still a potent healer. Love, love, love. Tender Love is the secret. Dwell on that thought - God is Love. Dwell on My actions on earth. See in them Love in operation. Remember:

- *God is Love . . . no judging.*
- *God is Love . . . no resentment.*
- *God is Love . . . all patience.*
- *God is Love . . . all power.*
- *God is Love . . . all supply.*

~

*J*ournaling *Your Journey* Spiritual insights - Conversations with God - Favorite verses - Prayers - Struggles, Joys...

_____

_____

_____

_____

_____

_____

_____

_____

This Week's Gratitude - Praise - Thanksgiving

✝✝✝

WEEK 24 - LIGHT

Jesus is Our Light

Monday

In the beginning was the Word,
and the Word was with God,
and the Word was God. . .
All things came into being by Him,
and apart from Him nothing came into being
that has come into being. In Him was life,
and the life was the light of men.
And the light shines in the darkness,
and the darkness did not comprehend it.
John 1:1,3-5 - NAS

_____

_____

_____

_____

_____

_____

_____

_____

_____

∾

Tuesday

Direct me in the path of your commands,
for there I find delight.
Turn my heart toward your statutes,
and not toward selfish gain.
Turn my eyes away from worthless things;
preserve my life according to your word

I gain understanding from your precepts;
therefore I hate every wrong path.
Your word is a lamp for my feet,
a light on my path.
Psalm 119:35-37;104-105 - NIV

~

Wednesday

This ... is the message which we have heard of him,
and declare unto you, that God is light,
and in him is no darkness at all.
1 John 1:5 - NAS

~

Thursday

God, who commanded the light to shine out of darkness,
hath shined in our hearts, to give the light of the knowledge
of the glory of God in the face of Jesus Christ.

2 Corinthians 4:6 - NAS

Friday
I have come into the world as a light,
so that no one who believes in me should stay in darkness.
John 12:46 - NAS

Saturday
For what fellowship has righteousness with lawlessness?
And what communion has light with darkness?
- For you were once darkness, but now you are light in the Lord.
Walk as children of light.
2 Corinthians 6:14; Ephesians 5:8 - NKJ

Sunday

Renew Me, O Eternal Light
And let my heart and soul be bright.
Illumined with the light of grace,
that issues from they holy face
Grant that I only Thee may love
And seek those things which are above
Till I behold Thee face to face,
O Light eternal, through they grace

Johanna F. Ruopp 1711

~

ournaling Your Journey Spiritual insights - Conversations
with God - Favorite verses - Prayers - Struggles, Joys...

_____
_____
_____
_____
_____
_____
_____
_____
_____
_____
_____
_____
_____
_____
_____
_____
_____
_____

This Week's Gratitude - Praise - Thanksgiving

_____
_____
_____
_____
_____
_____
_____
_____
_____
_____

✝✝✝

WEEK 25 - PRAISE GOD WITH JOY

THE LORD REIGNS, Let the Earth Rejoice – Psalm 97:1

Monday
Make a joyful noise to the Lord, all the earth;
break forth into joyous song and sing praises!
Sing praises to the Lord with the lyre,
with the lyre and the sound of melody!
With trumpets and the sound of the horn
make a joyful noise before the King, the Lord!
Psalm 98: 4-6 - ESV

～

Tuesday
Rejoice in the LORD, O you righteous! For praise from the upright is
beautiful. Psalm 33:1 - NKJ

_____
_____
_____
_____
_____

≈

Wednesday

As he was drawing near—already on the way down the Mount of Olives—the whole multitude of his disciples began to rejoice and praise God with a loud voice for all the mighty works that they had seen, saying, "Blessed is the King who comes in the name of the Lord! Peace in heaven and glory in the highest!"
Luke 19:37-38 - ESV

_____
_____
_____
_____
_____
_____
_____

≈

Thursday
Blessed are the people who know the joyful sound!
They walk, O LORD, in the light of Your countenance.
In Your name they rejoice all day long,
And in Your righteousness they are exalted.
For You are the glory of their strength,
And in Your favor our horn is exalted. Psalm 89:15-17 - NKJ

_____
_____
_____
_____
_____
_____
_____

≈

Friday

I have seen you in the sanctuary and beheld your power and your glory.
Because your love is better than life, my lips will glorify you.
I will praise you as long as I live, and in your name I will lift up my hands.
My soul will be satisfied as with the richest of foods;
with singing lips my mouth will praise you.
Psalm 63:2-5 - NIV

~

Saturday

Make a joyful noise to the Lord, all the earth!
Serve the Lord with gladness!
Come into his presence with singing!
Psalm 100:1 - ESV

~

Sunday

Praise to the Lord, the Almighty,
the King of creation!
O my soul praise Him,
for He is they Health and Salvation!
Join the full throng wake,
harp and psalter and song;
Sound forth in glad adoration!

Praise to the Lord!
Oh, let all that is in me adore Him!
All that has Life and breath -
come now with praises before Him!
Let the Amen - Sound from His people again;
Gladly for yes we adore Him.

Joachim Neander, 1679

~

*J***ournaling Your Journey** *Spiritual insights - Conversations with God - Favorite verses - Prayers - Struggles, Joys...*

_____
_____
_____
_____
_____
_____
_____
_____
_____
_____
_____
_____
_____
_____
_____
_____
_____

This Week's Gratitude - Praise - Thanksgiving

_____
_____
_____
_____
_____
_____
_____
_____
_____
_____
_____
_____

✝✝✝

WEEK 26 – REPLACE WORRY WITH FAITH

In the multitude of my anxieties within me, Your comforts delight my soul. Psalm 94:19

Monday

Do not be anxious about anything, but in everything, by prayer and petition, with thanksgiving, present your requests to God. And the peace of God, which transcends all understanding, will guard your hearts and your minds in Christ Jesus. Philippians 4:6-7 - NIV

_____

_____

_____

_____

_____

_____

_____

_____

~

Tuesday

Do not be anxious then, saying, 'What shall we eat?' or 'What shall we drink?' or 'With what shall we clothe ourselves?' -- for your heavenly Father knows that you need all these things. Matthew 6:31, 32 - NAS

_____

_____

_____

_____

_____

_____
_____
_____

~

Wednesday
But He said to them, "Why are you so fearful?
How is it that you have no faith?" - Perfect love casts out fear.
Mark 4:40; 1 John 4:18 - NKJ

_____
_____
_____
_____
_____
_____
_____

~

Thursday
"O our God, will You not judge them?
For we are powerless before this great multitude who are coming against us;
nor do we know what to do, but our eyes are on You." —
and he said, "Listen, all Judah and the inhabitants of Jerusalem
and King Jehoshaphat: thus says the Lord to you,
'Do not fear or be dismayed because of this great multitude,
for the battle is not yours but God's.'"
2 Chronicles 20:12,15 - KJV

_____
_____
_____
_____
_____
_____
_____

~

Friday
Are not two sparrows sold for a copper coin?
And not one of them falls to the ground apart from
your Father's will. But the very hairs of your head
are all numbered. Do not fear therefore;
you are of more value than many sparrows.
Matthew 10:29-31 - NKJ

_____

_____

_____

_____

_____

_____

_____

_____

~

Saturday
Whoever dwells in the shelter of the Most High
will rest in the shadow of the Almighty.
I will say of the Lord, "He is my refuge and my fortress,
my God, in whom I trust."
He will cover you with his feathers,
and under his wings you will find refuge;
his faithfulness will be your shield and rampart.
You will not fear the terror of night,
nor the arrow that flies by day,...
For he will command his angels concerning you
to guard you in all your ways;
they will lift you up in their hands,
so that you will not strike your foot against a stone.
Psalm 91:1-2,4-5,11-12 - NIV

_____

_____

_____

_____

_____

_____

_____

_____

~

<u>Sunday</u>

My hope is built on nothing less
Than Jesus Blood and Righteousness;
I dare not trust the sweetest frame,
But wholly lean on Jesus name.
On Christ the solid Rock I stand;
All other ground is sinking sand.

When darkness veils His lovely face,
I rest on His unchanging grace;
In every high and stormy gale
My anchor hold within the veil.
On Christ the solid Rock I stand;
All other ground is sinking sand.

Edward Mote, 1834

~

*J*ournaling Your Journey *Spiritual insights - Conversations with God -*
Favorite verses - Prayers - Struggles, Joys...

_____
_____
_____
_____
_____
_____
_____
_____
_____
_____
_____
_____
_____
_____
_____
_____

This Week's Gratitude - Praise - Thanksgiving

_____
_____
_____
_____
_____

_____
_____
_____
_____
_____
_____
_____
_____
_____
_____
_____

✝✝✝

WEEK 27 – GOD OUR STRENGTH I

God Lovingly Tends to Our Weaknesses

<u>Monday</u>
Do you not know? Have you not heard?
The LORD is the everlasting God,
the Creator of the ends of the earth.
He will not grow tired or weary,
and his understanding no one can fathom.

He gives power to the weak,
And to those who have no might He increases strength.
Even the youths shall faint and be weary,
And the young men shall utterly fall,
But those who wait on the Lord
Shall renew their strength;

They shall mount up with wings like eagles,
They shall run and not be weary,
They shall walk and not faint.
Isaiah 40:28-31 - NIV

Tuesday
Do not fear, for I am with you;
Do not anxiously look about you,
for I am your God.
I will strengthen you, surely I will help you,
Surely I will uphold you with
My righteous right hand.
Isaiah 41:10 - NAS

_____

_____

_____

_____

_____

_____

_____

~

Wednesday
Finally, my brethren, be strong in the Lord
and in the power of His might.
Ephesians 6:10 - NIV

_____

_____

_____

_____

_____

_____

_____

~

Thursday
Blessed is the man whose strength is in You,
Whose heart is set on pilgrimage.
As they pass through the Valley of Baca,
They make it a spring;
The rain also covers it with pools.
They go from strength to strength;
Each one appears before God in Zion.
Psalm 84:5-7 - NKJ

―――――――――――――――――――――――――
―――――――――――――――――――――――――
―――――――――――――――――――――――――
―――――――――――――――――――――――――
―――――――――――――――――――――――――
―――――――――――――――――――――――――
―――――――――――――――――――――――――
―――――――――――――――――――――――――

≈

Friday
I will seek what was lost and bring back
what was driven away,
bind up the broken and strengthen
what was sick.
Ezekiel 34:16 - NKJ

―――――――――――――――――――――――――
―――――――――――――――――――――――――
―――――――――――――――――――――――――
―――――――――――――――――――――――――
―――――――――――――――――――――――――
―――――――――――――――――――――――――
―――――――――――――――――――――――――
―――――――――――――――――――――――――

≈

Saturday
In quietness and trust is your strength -
Wait for the LORD; Be strong,
and let your heart take courage;
Yes, wait for the LORD.
Isaiah 30:15, Psalm 27:14 - NAS

―――――――――――――――――――――――――
―――――――――――――――――――――――――
―――――――――――――――――――――――――
―――――――――――――――――――――――――
―――――――――――――――――――――――――
―――――――――――――――――――――――――
―――――――――――――――――――――――――
―――――――――――――――――――――――――

≈

Sunday

The Two Listeners

You do not realize that you would have broken down under the weight of your care but for the renewing time with Me. It is not what I say; it is I, Myself. It is not the hearing Me so much as the being in my Presence. The strengthening and curative powers of this you cannot know. Such knowledge is beyond your human reckoning. . .

Oh, Joy that I am with you. For this I came to Earth, to lead man back to spirit-converse with his God.

❧

*J***ournaling Your Journey** *Spiritual insights - Conversations with God - Favorite verses - Prayers - Struggles, Joys...*

_____
_____
_____
_____
_____
_____
_____
_____
_____
_____
_____
_____
_____
_____
_____
_____
_____

This Week's Gratitude - Praise - Thanksgiving

_____
_____
_____
_____
_____
_____
_____
_____
_____
_____

✝✝✝

WEEK 28 – GOD OUR STRENGTH II

Our Strength is in Him – Not in Ourselves

Monday
*If anyone speaks, he should do it as one speaking the very words of God.
If anyone serves, he should do it with the strength God provides,
so that in all things God may be praised through Jesus Christ.
To him be the glory and the power for ever and ever. Amen
1 Peter 4:11 - NIV*

_____

_____

_____

_____

_____

_____

_____

_____

~

Tuesday
*The Lord is my strength and my shield; My heart trusts in Him,
and I am helped; Therefore my heart exults, and with my song
I shall thank Him. - The Lord will give strength to His people;
The Lord will bless His people with peace.
Psalms 28:7; 29:11 - NAS*

_____

_____

_____
_____
_____
_____
_____
_____
_____

~

Wednesday
Be of good courage, And He shall strengthen your heart,
All you who hope in the LORD.
Look to the LORD and his strength;
seek his face always. Psalms 31:24;105:4 - NIV

_____
_____
_____
_____
_____
_____
_____
_____

~

Thursday
For You have been a strength to the poor,
A strength to the needy in his distress,
A refuge from the storm,
A shade from the heat;
For the blast of the terrible ones
is as a storm against the wall.
Isaiah 25:4 - NKJ

_____
_____
_____
_____
_____
_____
_____

~

Friday

Strength and dignity are her clothing, and she smiles at the future.
She opens her mouth in wisdom, and the teaching of kindness is on her tongue.
Proverbs 31:25-26 - NAS

_____

_____

_____

_____

_____

_____

_____

_____

∽

Saturday

After you have suffered for a little while, the God of all grace
[who imparts His blessing and favor], who called you to His own eternal glory
in Christ, will Himself complete, confirm, strengthen, and establish you
[making you what you ought to be].
1 Peter 5:10 - AMP

_____

_____

_____

_____

_____

_____

_____

∽

Sunday

Prayer

Eternal God, have mercy on me, and protect me from bitterness, confusion,
suffering, disappointments in this world. Give me an unwavering faith which
will hold fast to Jesus Christ as my Savior and Friend.

Lift me to Yourself, and let Your Holy Spirit breath into my heart the joy of
forgiveness and peace. Strengthen my faith. Guard me against the temptations
that easily beset me or a peevish attitude. And make me hopeful, confident,
cheerful, and courageous in You! I ask this in the name and for the sake of
Jesus Christ, my Lord. Amen

~

*J*ournaling **Your Journey** *Spiritual insights - Conversations with God - Favorite verses - Prayers - Struggles, Joys...*

_____
_____
_____
_____
_____
_____
_____
_____
_____
_____
_____
_____
_____
_____
_____
_____

This Week's Gratitude - Praise - Thanksgiving

_____
_____
_____
_____
_____
_____
_____
_____
_____
_____
_____
_____
_____
_____

✝✝✝

WEEK 29 – ETERNITY VS. TIME

Blessed is the man whose strength is in You, whose heart is set on pilgrimage. Psalm 84:5

Monday

For our light and momentary troubles are achieving for us an eternal glory that far outweighs them all. So we fix our eyes not on what is seen, but on what is unseen. For what is seen is temporary, but what is unseen is eternal.
2 corinthians 4:17-18 - NIV

~

Tuesday

For here we do not have a lasting city,
but we are seeking the city
which is to come. Through Him then, let us continually offer
up a sacrifice of praise to God, that is,
the fruit of lips that give thanks to His name.
Hebrews 13:14-15 - NAS

~

Wednesday
I consider that our present sufferings are not worth
comparing with the glory that will be revealed in us.
- Fear not, little flock; for it is your
Father's good pleasure to give you the kingdom.
Romans 8:18 - NIV ; Luke 12:32 - KJV

~

Thursday
But now having been set free from sin,
and having become slaves of God,
you have fruit to holiness, and the end,
everlasting life. - For he who sows to his flesh
will of the flesh reap corruption, but he who sows to the
Spirit will of the Spirit reap everlasting life.
Romans 6:22; Galatians 6:8 - NKJ

~

<u>Friday</u>

- *Your work, O LORD, is eternal; it stands firm in the heavens. Psalm 119:89 - NIV*
- *The eternal God is a dwelling place, and underneath are the everlasting arms;... Deuteronomy 33:27 - NAS*
- *But the LORD is the true God; He is the living God and the everlasting King. Jeremiah 10:10 - NAS*
- *Now this is eternal life, that they may know you, the only true God, and Jesus Christ, whom you have sent. John 17:3 - NAS*
- *But whoever drinks of the water that I will give him shall never thirst; but the water that I will give him will become in him a well of water springing up to eternal life. John 4:14 - NAS*

_____
_____
_____
_____
_____
_____
_____

∼

<u>Saturday</u>
*... He will wipe away every tear from their eyes;
and there will no longer be any death;
there will no longer be any mourning, or crying,
or pain; the first things have passed away.
Revelation 21:4 - NAS*

_____
_____
_____
_____
_____
_____

∼

<u>Sunday</u>

I know God wont give me anything I can't handle,

I just wish He didn't trust me so much!

— MOTHER TERESA

Have courage for the great sorrows of life and patience for the small ones; and when you have laboriously accomplished your daily task, go to sleep in peace. God is awake.

— VICTOR HUGO

Prayer
Lord, Please give me an eye to see all things in this life from an eternal perspective, to understand that pursuing personal passions apart from Your will is loss.

Help me treasure my quiet devotional time with You as the highlight of my day, and help me display Your love to those around me so that they may come to know You.

I ask for eternal fruit in my life, and trust that You will show me next steps for rendering it. I thank You for showing me how delightful simplicity in You is a blessing, and I praise You for all Your care and protection! In Jesus Name, Amen

~

*J*ournaling Your Journey *Spiritual insights - Conversations with God - Favorite verses - Prayers - Struggles, Joys...*

_____
_____
_____
_____
_____
_____
_____
_____
_____
_____
_____
_____
_____
_____

_____
_____
_____
_____

This Week's Gratitude - Praise - Thanksgiving

_____
_____
_____
_____
_____
_____
_____
_____
_____
_____
_____
_____
_____
_____

✝✝✝

WEEK 30 – THIS IS NOT YOUR REST

Relying on Anything Else But God

Monday
Arise and go, for this is no place of rest. Because of the uncleanness that brings on destruction, a painful destruction. Micah 2:10 - NAS

_____
_____
_____
_____
_____
_____
_____
_____

∼

Tuesday
Do not be carried away by varied and strange teachings; for it is good for the heart to be strengthened by grace. . . - Hebrews 13:9 - NAS

_____
_____
_____
_____
_____
_____
_____
_____

Wednesday

So that we are no longer children [spiritually immature], tossed back and forth [like ships on a stormy sea] and carried about by every wind of [shifting] doctrine, by the cunning and trickery of [unscrupulous] men, by the deceitful scheming of people ready to do anything [for personal profit]. But speaking the truth in love [in all things—both our speech and our lives expressing His truth], let us grow up in all things into Him [following His example] who is the Head—Christ. Ephesians 4:14-15 - AMP

∾

Thursday

Who is among you who fears the Lord,
Who obeys the voice of His Servant,
Yet who walks in darkness and has no light?
Let him trust and be confident in the name of the Lord
and let him rely on his God.

Listen carefully, all you who kindle your own fire
[devising your own man-made plan of salvation],
Who surround yourselves with torches,
Walk by the light of your [self-made] fire
And among the torches that you have set ablaze.
But this you will have from My hand:
You will lie down in [a place of] torment.
Isaiah 50:10-11 - AMP

∾

Friday
So put to death and deprive of power the evil longings of your earthly body
[with its sensual, self-centered instincts] immorality, impurity, sinful passion,
evil desire, and greed, which is [a kind of] idolatry [because it replaces your
devotion to God]. Colossians 3:5 - AMP

_____

_____

_____

_____

_____

_____

_____

_____

~

Saturday
But the wicked are like the tossing sea,
For it cannot be quiet,
And its waters toss up refuse and mud.
"There is no peace," says my God, "for the wicked."
Isaiah 57:20, 21 - NAS

_____

_____

_____

_____

_____

_____

_____

~

Sunday

The Two Listeners
The world sees strength in action. In My Kingdom it is known that strength
lies in quiet. "In quietness and in confidence shall be your strength." All you
have 'missed' you will find in Me, the soul's Lover, the soul's Friend, Father –
Comrade – Brother. Try Me.

~

*J*ournaling **Your Journey** *Spiritual insights - Conversations with God - Favorite verses - Prayers - Struggles, Joys...*

_____
_____
_____
_____
_____
_____
_____
_____
_____
_____
_____
_____
_____
_____
_____
_____
_____

This Week's Gratitude - Praise - Thanksgiving

_____
_____
_____
_____
_____
_____
_____
_____
_____
_____
_____
_____
_____
_____

✝✝✝

WEEK 31 – JESUS

Jesus my Shepherd, Guardian, Friend; My Prophet, Priest, & King; My Lord, my Life, my Way my End, Accept the praise I bring. - John Newton 1779

Monday
Jesus the author and perfecter of our faith.
And by that will, we have been made holy
through the sacrifice of the body of Jesus
Christ once for all. But when this priest had offered for all time
one sacrifice for sins, he sat down at the right hand of God.
Since that time he waits for his enemies
to be made his footstool.
Hebrews 10:2,10,12 - NIV

_____
_____
_____
_____
_____
_____
_____
_____
_____

∼

Tuesday

Greater love has no man than this,
that a man lay down his life for his friends. —
For the life of the flesh is in the blood, and I have given it to you
upon the altar to make atonement for your souls;
for it is the blood that makes atonement for the soul.
John 15:13; Leviticus 17:11- KJV

_____

_____

_____

_____

_____

_____

_____

~

Wednesday

Behold! The Lamb of God who takes away the sin of the world! —
Jesus said, "It is finished." With that, he bowed his head and gave up
his spirit. — by one sacrifice he has made perfect forever those who are
being made holy. John 1:29,19:30; Hebrews 10:14 - NIV

_____

_____

_____

_____

_____

_____

_____

~

Thursday

— having canceled out the certificate of debt consisting of legal demands
[which were in force] against us and which were hostile to us.
And this certificate He has set aside and completely removed
by nailing it to the cross. Colossians 2:14 - AMP

_____

_____

_____

_____

―――――――――――――――――――――――――――――――――
―――――――――――――――――――――――――――――――――
―――――――――――――――――――――――――――――――――
―――――――――――――――――――――――――――――――――
―――――――――――――――――――――――――――――――――

~

Friday

I lay down My life that I may take it again. No one has taken it away from Me, but I lay it down on My own initiative. I have authority to lay it down, and I have authority to take it up again. This commandment I received from My Father. John 10:17, 18 - NAS

―――――――――――――――――――――――――――――――――
―――――――――――――――――――――――――――――――――
―――――――――――――――――――――――――――――――――
―――――――――――――――――――――――――――――――――
―――――――――――――――――――――――――――――――――
―――――――――――――――――――――――――――――――――
―――――――――――――――――――――――――――――――――

~

Saturday

*The Spirit of the Lord God is upon me,
Because the LORD has anointed me to bring good news to the afflicted;
He has sent me to bind up the brokenhearted,
To proclaim liberty to captives, And freedom to prisoners; . . .*

To grant those who mourn *in* Zion,
giving them a garland instead of ashes, the oil of gladness instead of mourning, the mantle of praise instead of a spirit of fainting.
So they will be called oaks of righteousness,
The planting of the Lord, that He may be glorified.
Isaiah 61:1,3 - NAS

―――――――――――――――――――――――――――――――――
―――――――――――――――――――――――――――――――――
―――――――――――――――――――――――――――――――――
―――――――――――――――――――――――――――――――――
―――――――――――――――――――――――――――――――――
―――――――――――――――――――――――――――――――――
―――――――――――――――――――――――――――――――――
―――――――――――――――――――――――――――――――――

Sunday

Let us ever walk with Jesus,
Follow His example pure,
Flee the world, which would deceive us -
And to sin our souls allure.
Ever in His footsteps treading,
Body here, yet soul above,
Full of faith and hope an love,
Let us do the Father's bidding.
Faithful Lord, abide with me;
Savior, lead I follow Thee.

Sigismund von Birken, 1653

∾

Journaling Your Journey Spiritual insights - Conversations with God - Favorite verses - Prayers - Struggles, Joys...

_____
_____
_____
_____
_____
_____
_____
_____
_____
_____
_____
_____
_____
_____
_____
_____
_____

This Week's Gratitude - Praise - Thanksgiving

_____
_____
_____
_____
_____
_____
_____
_____

✝✝✝

WEEK 32 – FRUIT OF GOODNESS

"You are my Lord, my goodness is nothing apart from You." –– Psalms 16:2

Monday
The fruit of the Spirit is … goodness. Galatians 5:27 - KJV

_____
_____
_____
_____
_____
_____
_____
_____

~

Tuesday
But I tell you: Love your enemies and pray for those who persecute you, that you may be sons of your Father in heaven. He causes his sun to rise on the evil and the good, and sends rain on the righteous and the unrighteous.
Matthew 5:44, 45 - NIV

_____
_____
_____
_____
_____
_____
_____

Wednesday
Surely Your goodness and Love will follow me all the days of my life — Be merciful, just as your Father is merciful. Psalm 23:6; Luke 6:36 - NIV

∾

Thursday
After that the kindness and love of God our Savior toward man appeared, not by works of righteousness which we have done, but according to his mercy he saved us, by the washing of regeneration, and renewing of the Holy Ghost; which he shed on us abundantly through Jesus Christ our Savior.
Titus 3:4-6 - KJV

∾

Friday
The LORD is good to all; he has compassion on all he has made.
Psalm 145:9 - NIV

Saturday

The fruit of the Spirit is in all goodness and righteousness and truth. Be ... followers of God, as dear children. Ephesians 5:9,1 - KJV

≈

Sunday

A Christian should always remember that the value of his good works is not based on their number and excellence, but on the love of God that prompts him to do these things.

— JOHN OF THE CROSS

≈

Journaling Your Journey Spiritual insights - Conversations with God - Favorite verses - Prayers - Struggles, Joys...

This Week's Gratitude - Praise - Thanksgiving

✝✝✝

WEEK 33 – CREATOR

Let them praise the name of the Lord, For He commanded and they were created. Psalms 148:5

Monday
In the beginning God created the heavens and the earth.
— For in six days the Lord made the heavens and the earth,
the sea and all that is in them, and rested on the seventh day;
therefore the Lord blessed the sabbath day and made it holy.
Genesis 1:1; Exodus 20:11 - NAS

_____
_____
_____
_____
_____
_____
_____
_____

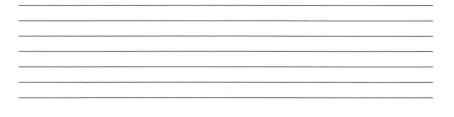

Tuesday
The heavens are telling of the glory of God;
And their expanse is declaring the work of His hands. —

O Lord, our Lord, How majestic is Your name in all the earth,
Who have displayed Your splendor above the heavens! …

When I consider Your heavens, the work of Your fingers,
The moon and the stars, which You have ordained;

What is man that You take thought of him,
And the son of man that You care for him?
Psalms 19:1;8:1,3, 4 - NAS

∾

Wednesday

By faith we understand that the worlds were prepared
by the word of God, so that what is seen was not made
out of things which are visible.
— By the word of the Lord the heavens were made,
And by the breath of His mouth all their host.

He gathers the waters of the sea together as a heap;
He lays up the deeps in storehouses.
Let all the earth fear the Lord;
Let all the inhabitants of the world stand in awe of Him.
For He spoke, and it was done;
He commanded, and it stood fast.
Hebrews 11:3; Psalm 33:6-9 - NAS

∾

Thursday

In the beginning was the Word,
and the Word was with God,
and the Word was God.
He was in the beginning with God.
All things came into being by Him,
and apart from Him nothing came into being
that has come into being.
John 1:1-2 - NAS

∾

Friday

Bless the Lord, O my soul! O Lord my God, you are very great;
You are clothed with splendor and majesty, covering Yourself with light
as with a cloak, stretching out heaven like a tent curtain.

He lays the beams of His upper chambers in the waters;
He makes the clouds His chariot; He walks upon the wings of the wind;
He makes the winds His messengers, Flaming fire His ministers.

He established the earth upon its foundations,
so that it will not totter forever and ever.
Psalm 104: 1-5 - NAS

∾

Saturday

Lift up your eyes on high And see who has created these stars, The One who leads forth their host by number, He calls them all by name; Because of the greatness of His might and the strength of His power, Not one of them is missing. Isaiah 40:26 - NAS

"Drip down, O heavens, from above, and let the clouds pour down righteousness; Let the earth open up and salvation bear fruit, and righteousness spring up with it. I, the Lord, have created it.

It is I who made the earth, and created man upon it. I stretched out the heavens with My hands And I ordained all their host.

I have aroused him in righteousness and I will make all his ways smooth; He will build My city and will let My exiles go free, Without any payment or reward," says the Lord of hosts. Isaiah 45:8,12-13 - NAS

_____

_____

_____

_____

_____

_____

_____

_____

~

Sunday

Prayer

Our help, O Lord, comes from You, who made heaven and earth! We lift up our joyful praise to You from Whom all blessings flow! Our hearts are delighted by communion with Your Spirit, and in the Light of Your presence we walk all the day. We overflow with gratitude for Your protection and strength throughout this past week. As we lie down and rest, You keep us safe.

On eagles wings You both carry and shelter us. O Lord, we love You dearly! Our time, our life, our salvation, O mighty and merciful God are in Your hands. We know in Who we believe and to You we commit our bodies and souls for safekeeping in time and eternity. In Jesus' name. Amen

~

*J**ournaling Your Journey** Spiritual insights - Conversations with God - Favorite verses - Prayers - Struggles, Joys...*

_____
_____
_____
_____
_____
_____
_____
_____
_____
_____
_____
_____
_____
_____
_____
_____
_____

This Week's Gratitude - Praise - Thanksgiving

_____
_____
_____
_____
_____
_____
_____
_____
_____
_____
_____
_____
_____
_____
_____

✟✟✟

WEEK 34 – YOU ARE GOD'S TEMPLE

In whom you also are being built together into a dwelling of God in the Spirit. Ephesians 2:22 - NAS

Monday
Your body is the temple of the Holy Spirit which is in you.
1 Corinthians 6:19 - NKJ

_____
_____
_____
_____
_____
_____
_____
_____

∾

Tuesday
Jesus answered and said to him, "If anyone loves Me, he will keep My word; and My Father will love him, and We will come to him and make Our abode with him." John 14:23 — NAS

_____
_____
_____
_____
_____
_____

Wednesday
For we are the temple of the living God; just as God said,
"I will dwell in them and walk among them;
And I will be their God, and they shall be My people."
2 Corinthians 6:16 - NAS

_____
_____
_____
_____
_____
_____
_____
_____

~

Thursday
Abide in Me, and I in you. . .
I am the vine, you are the branches; he who abides in Me and I in him, he
bears much fruit, for apart from Me you can do nothing.
If you abide in Me, and My words abide in you, ask whatever you wish, and it
will be done for you.

Just as the Father has loved Me, I have also loved you; abide in My love.
If you keep My commandments, you will abide in My love; just as I have
kept My Father's commandments and abide in His love.
John 15:4,5,7,9-10 - NAS

_____
_____
_____
_____
_____
_____
_____
_____

~

Friday
Let them make me a sanctuary; that I may dwell among them. . . I will meet
with the children of Israel, and the tabernacle shall be sanctified by my glory.
And I will dwell among the children of Israel, and will be their God.
Exodus 25:8; 29:43, 45 - KJV

_____
_____
_____
_____
_____
_____
_____
_____

~

Saturday

Therefore, brothers, since we have confidence to enter the Most Holy Place by the blood of Jesus, by a new and living way . . ., let us draw near to God with a sincere heart in full assurance of faith, having our hearts sprinkled to cleanse us from a guilty conscience and having our bodies washed with pure water. Hebrews 10:19-22 - NIV

_____
_____
_____
_____
_____
_____
_____

~

Sunday

That practice which is alike the most holy... and the most needful in the spiritual life is the practice of the Presence of God. It is the schooling of the soul to find its joy in His Divine Companionship.

— BROTHER LAWRENCE, 17TH CENTURY

The Two Listeners
Cling to Me. Stick fast to Me. Live the life of close and intimate communion with Me. Get nearer to Me. Roll every burden on Me. Cast your whole weight on Me. Never let go your hold on Me for a moment. Be, as it were, rooted and planted in Me. Do this and I will ever abide in you.

*J*ournaling Your Journey *Spiritual insights - Conversations with God - Favorite verses - Prayers - Struggles, Joys...*

_____
_____
_____
_____
_____
_____
_____
_____
_____
_____
_____
_____
_____
_____
_____
_____

This Week's Gratitude - Praise - Thanksgiving

_____
_____
_____
_____
_____
_____
_____
_____
_____
_____
_____
_____
_____
_____
_____

✝✝✝

WEEK 35 – THE LORD DELIGHTS IN YOU!

Delight Also in Him

Monday
For the LORD delights in you, Isaiah 62:4 - NKJ

The Lord your God is with you, the Mighty Warrior who saves.
He will take great delight in you; in his love he will no longer rebuke you,
but will rejoice over you with singing. Zephaniah 3:17 — NIV

_____
_____
_____
_____
_____
_____
_____
_____
_____

~

Tuesday
The LORD delights in those who…, who put their hope in his unfailing love.
Psalm 147:11 - NIV

_____
_____
_____
_____
_____

_____
_____
_____

∾

Wednesday
I sat down under his shadow with great delight,
and his fruit was sweet to my taste.
He brought me to the banqueting house,
and his banner over me was love.
Song of Songs 2:3, 4 - KJV

_____
_____
_____
_____
_____
_____
_____

∾

Thursday
"My delights were with the sons of men."
— looking unto Jesus, the author and finisher of our faith,
who for the joy that was set before Him endured the cross, despising
the shame,
and has sat down at the right hand of the throne of God.
Proverbs 8:31; Hebrews 12:2 - KJV

_____
_____
_____
_____
_____
_____
_____

∾

Friday

The steps of a good man are ordered by the LORD:
and he delights in his way.
Psalm 37:23 -NKJ

_____
_____
_____
_____
_____
_____
_____
_____
_____

~

Saturday

They shall be Mine, says the LORD of hosts, On the day that I make them My
jewels. And I will spare them As a man spares his own son who serves him.
Malachi 3:17 - NKJ

_____
_____
_____
_____
_____
_____
_____
_____

~

Sunday

Prayer

My Father, as Your child, I am encouraged when thinking how You delight in
me. Your Fatherly joy fills my heart with warmth. As my loving Father, You
smile lovingly and rejoice even over my small steps. When I stumble learning
from my mistakes, Your compassion brings comfort and assurance. Your
Delight in me brings joy and gladness!

Let me ever be thankful that You drew me with bands of kindness, that Your
love for me is assured. Help me to draw nearer to You. Show me how I may
walk even closer to You day by day, opening my eyes to see even more clearly
Your delight and peace. Amen

*J*ournaling *Your Journey* *Spiritual insights - Conversations with God -*
Favorite verses - Prayers - Struggles, Joys...

_____
_____
_____
_____
_____
_____
_____
_____
_____
_____
_____
_____
_____
_____
_____
_____

This Week's Gratitude - Praise - Thanksgiving

_____
_____
_____
_____
_____
_____
_____
_____
_____
_____
_____
_____
_____
_____
_____

✝✝✝

WEEK 36 - LOVE FOR GOD

Loving God is our greatest joy, He abides with those who love Him .
— John 15

Monday
"Teacher, which is the greatest commandment in the Law?" Jesus replied: "'Love the Lord your God with all your heart and with all your soul and with all your mind. This is the first and greatest commandment." Matthew 22:36-37 - NIV

_____

_____

_____

_____

_____

_____

_____

~

Tuesday
Only be very careful to observe the commandment and the law which Moses the servant of the LORD commanded you, to love the LORD your God and walk in all His ways and keep His commandments and hold fast to Him and serve Him with all your heart and with all your soul.
Joshua 22:5 - NAS

_____

_____

_____
_____
_____
_____
_____
_____

❀

Wednesday

O love the LORD, all you His godly ones!
The LORD preserves the faithful,
And fully recompenses the proud doer.
Be strong, and let your heart take courage,
All you who hope in the LORD.
Psalm 31: 23-24 - NAS

_____
_____
_____
_____
_____
_____
_____

❀

Thursday

I Love you, O LORD, my strength. The LORD is my rock and my
fortress and my deliverer, My God, my rock, in whom I take refuge; My
shield and the horn of my salvation, my stronghold. Psalm
18:1-2 - ESV

_____
_____
_____
_____
_____
_____
_____

❀

Friday

If anyone says, "I love God," and hates his brother, he is a liar; for the one who does not love his brother whom he has seen, cannot love God whom he has not seen. And this commandment we have from Him; whoever loves God must also love his brother. 1 John 4:20-21 - ESV

_____
_____
_____
_____
_____
_____
_____
_____

Saturday

So when they had finished breakfast, Jesus said to Simon Peter, "Simon, son of John, do you love Me more than these?" He said to Him, "Yes, Lord; You know that I love You." He said to him, "Tend My lambs." . . . "Shepherd My sheep." . . . "Tend My sheep." John 21: 15-17 - NAS

_____
_____
_____
_____
_____
_____
_____
_____

Sunday

PRAYER OF ST. RICHARD OF CHICHESTER
*Most merciful Redeemer, Friend and Brother,
may we know you more clearly,
love you more dearly,
and follow you more nearly,
day by day.
Amen.*

Thee will I love, my Strength and Tower;
Thee will I love, my Hope, my Joy;
Thee will I love and praise forever,
For never shall Thy kindness end;
Thee will I love, O Light Divine,
So long as life is mine.

Johann Schaffer, 1657

*J**ournaling Your Journey** Spiritual insights - Conversations with God -*
Favorite verses - Prayers - Struggles, Joys...

This Week's Gratitude - Praise - Thanksgiving

WEEK 37 – LOVE FOR OTHERS

... and they will know we are christ's followers by our love

Monday
A new command I give you:
Love one another.
As I have loved you,
so you must love one another.
By this all men will know that you are my disciples,
if you love one another.
John 13:34-35 - NIV

_____

_____

_____

_____

_____

_____

_____

_____

_____

~

Tuesday
— Walk in a manner worthy of the calling to which you have been called,
with all humility and gentleness, with patience,
bearing with one another in love,
eager to maintain the unity of the Spirit
in the bond of peace.
Ephesians 4:1-3 - ESV

~

Wednesday
For you were called to freedom, brethren;
only do not turn your freedom into an opportunity for the flesh,
but through love serve one another. For the whole Law is fulfilled in
one word, in the statement, "You shall love your neighbor as yourself."
But if you bite and devour one another, take care lest you be consumed
by one another. But I say, walk by the Spirit, and you will not carry
out the desire of the flesh. Galatians 5:13-16 - NAS

~

Thursday
Let no debt remain outstanding, except the continuing debt to love one
another, for he who loves his fellowman has fulfilled the law.
Romans 13:8 - NIV

~

Friday
Beloved, let us love one another, for love is of God;
and everyone who loves is born of God and knows God.
He who does not love does not know God, for God is love.
Beloved, if God so loved us, we also ought to love one another.
No one has seen God at any time. If we love one another, God abides in us,
and His love has been perfected in us.
1 John 4:7-8; 11-12 - NKJ

~

Saturday
Having purified your souls by your obedience to the truth for a sincere
brotherly love, love one another earnestly from a pure heart, since you
have been born again, not of perishable seed but of imperishable,
through the living and abiding word of God. 1 Peter 1:22-23 - ESV

~

Sunday

"Whatever a person may be like, we must still love them because we love God."

— JOHN CALVIN

Prayer

Heavenly Father, Cleanse my heart of all ill will toward those I encounter during my daily life. Help me to walk in the purity of Your love so I may shine the light of Your love to others. As You are the author of love I ask for You to teach me how — open my eyes to see and my ears to hear Your gentle leading. In Jesus name, Amen

～

*J*ournaling Your Journey *Spiritual insights - Conversations with God - Favorite verses - Prayers - Struggles, Joys...*

_____
_____
_____
_____
_____
_____
_____
_____
_____
_____
_____
_____
_____
_____
_____
_____

This Week's Gratitude - Praise - Thanksgiving

_____
_____
_____
_____
_____
_____
_____

_____

✝✝✝

WEEK 38 – HEARING

Hearing the truth will set you free – "those who have ears, let them hear" with heart & mind

Monday
Then a cloud formed, overshadowing them,
and a voice came out of the cloud,
"This is My beloved Son, listen to Him!"
— Faith comes from hearing the message,
and the message is heard through the word of Christ.
Matthew 9:7; Romans 10:17 - NIV

_____
_____
_____
_____
_____
_____
_____

~

Tuesday
The wind blows wherever it pleases. You hear its sound, but you cannot tell
where it comes from or where it is going. So it is with everyone born of the
Spirit. John 3:8 - NIV

_____
_____
_____

_____
_____
_____
_____
_____
_____

∽

Wednesday
Let me hear Thy lovingkindness in the morning; For I trust in Thee;
Teach me the way in which I should walk; For to Thee I lift up my soul.
Psalm 143:8 - NAS

_____
_____
_____
_____
_____
_____
_____
_____

∽

Thursday
"The sower sows the word. . . these are the ones sown on good ground,
those who hear the word, accept it, and bear fruit:
If anyone has ears to hear, let him hear."
Also He said to them, "Take heed what you hear...."
Mark 4:14,20,23,24

_____
_____
_____
_____
_____
_____
_____
_____

∽

Friday

The Lord God has given Me the tongue of disciples, That I may know how to sustain the weary one with a word. He awakens Me morning by morning, He awakens My ear to listen as a disciple. The Lord God has opened My ear. — And your ears will hear a word behind you, "This is the way, walk in it," whenever you turn to the right or to the left.
Isaiah 50:4-5;30:21 - NAS

≈

Saturday

But prove yourselves doers of the word [actively and continually obeying God's precepts], and not merely listeners [who hear the word but fail to internalize its meaning], deluding yourselves [by unsound reasoning contrary to the truth].

For if anyone only listens to the word without obeying it, he is like a man who looks very carefully at his natural face in a mirror; for once he has looked at himself and gone away, he immediately forgets what he looked like.

But he who looks carefully into the perfect law, the law of liberty, and faithfully abides by it, not having become a [careless] listener who forgets but an active doer [who obeys], he will be blessed and favored by God in what he does [in his life of obedience]. James 1:22-25 - AMP

≈

<u>Sunday</u>
Come, very Sun of truth and love,
Come in Your radiance from above
And shed the Holy Spirit's ray
On all we think or do today.

Direct and govern heart and mind,
With body chaste and disciplined;
Let faith her eager fires renew
And hate the false and love the true.

St. Ambrose, 397

~

ournaling Your Journey *Spiritual insights - Conversations with God -*
Favorite verses - Prayers - Struggles, Joys...

_____
_____
_____
_____
_____
_____
_____
_____
_____
_____
_____
_____
_____
_____
_____
_____

This Week's Gratitude - Praise - Thanksgiving

_____
_____
_____
_____
_____
_____
_____
_____

_____
_____
_____
_____
_____
_____

✝✝✝

WEEK 39 – TRUE REST IN GOD

Take My yoke upon you and learn from Me, for I am gentle and
humble in heart, and you will find rest for your souls. Matthew 11:29

Monday
*For we who have believed enter that rest,... For the one who has entered His
rest has himself also rested from his works, - Let us therefore be diligent to
enter that rest, lest anyone fall through following the same example of
disobedience. Hebrews 4:3,10-11 - NAS*

_____
_____
_____
_____
_____
_____
_____

∽

Tuesday
*Come unto me, all ye that labour and are heavy laden,
and I will give you rest. Matthew 11:28 - KJV*

_____
_____
_____
_____
_____
_____

Wednesday

If you keep your feet from breaking the Sabbath
and from doing as you please on my holy day,
if you call the Sabbath a delight
and the LORD's holy day honorable,
and if you honor it by not going your own way
and not doing as you please or speaking idle words,
then you will find your joy in the LORD.
Isaiah 58:13,14 - NIV

∾

Thursday

This is what the LORD says: "Stand at the crossroads and look; ask for the
ancient paths, ask where the good way is, and walk in it, and you will find rest
for your souls." Jeremiah 6:16 - NIV

∾

Friday

Trust in the LORD, and do good;
Dwell in the land and cultivate faithfulness.
Delight yourself in the LORD;
And He will give you the desires of your heart.
Commit your way to the LORD,
Trust also in Him, and He will do it. ...

Rest in the LORD and wait patiently for Him;

Do not fret because of him who prospers in his way,
Because of the man who carries out wicked schemes.
Cease from anger, and forsake wrath;
Do not fret, it leads only to evildoing.
Psalm 37:3-5;7-8 - KJV

~

Saturday
He makes me to lie down in green pastures;
He leads me beside the still waters.
He restores my soul --
Psalm 23:2-3 - NKJ

~

Sunday

The Two Listeners
Rest in Me... Rest then until My Life-Power flows through you. Have no fear
for the future. Be quiet, be still, and in that very stillness your strength will
come and will be maintained. To see Me you must bring Me your cares and
show Me your heart of trust. Then as you leave your cares you become
conscience of My presence... True Love and Peace to overflowing.

~

*J*ournaling Your Journey *Spiritual insights - Conversations with God - Favorite verses - Prayers - Struggles, Joys...*

_____
_____
_____
_____
_____
_____
_____
_____
_____
_____
_____
_____
_____
_____
_____
_____
_____

This Week's Gratitude - Praise - Thanksgiving

_____
_____
_____
_____
_____
_____
_____
_____
_____
_____
_____
_____
_____
_____
_____

✝✝✝

WEEK 40 – SEEKING

Ask, and it will be given to you; seek, and you will find; knock, and it will be opened to you. For everyone who asks receives, and he who seeks finds, and to him who knocks it will be opened. Matthew 7:7-8

Monday
As the deer pants for streams of water, so my soul pants for you, O God. My soul thirsts for God, for the living God.

— Let the light of your face shine upon us, O LORD! You have filled my heart with greater joy than when their grain and new wine abound.

Psalm 42:1, 2 - NIV; Psalm 4:6,7 - NAS

_____

_____

_____

_____

_____

_____

_____

_____

Tuesday

You will seek me and find me when you seek me with all you heart.
— [Hidden Treasure] "The kingdom of heaven is like a treasure
hidden in the field, which a man found and hid again; and from joy
over it he goes and sells all that he has and buys that field.
Jeremiah 29;13; Matthew 13:44 - NAS

∾

Wednesday

Mary . . . sat at Jesus' feet, and heard his word. "One thing is needful."
— One thing have I desired of the LORD, that will I seek after; that I
may dwell in the house of the LORD all the days of my life, to behold
the beauty of the Lord, and to enquire in his temple.
Luke 10:39,42; Psalm 27:4 - KJV

∾

Thursday

[*The Lost Coin*] Or what woman, if she has ten silver coins and loses
one coin, does not light a lamp and sweep the house and search
carefully until she finds it? — "I have not departed from the
command of His lips; I have treasured the words of His mouth more
than my necessary food." Luke 15:8; Job 23:12 - NAS

_____
_____
_____
_____
_____

~

Friday
Jesus said to them, "I am the bread of life; he who comes to Me shall not hunger, and he who believes in Me shall never thirst." John 6:35 - NAS

_____
_____
_____
_____
_____
_____
_____

~

Saturday
O God, You are my God; Early will I seek You; My soul thirsts for You; My flesh longs for You in a dry and thirsty land where there is no water. So I have looked for You in the sanctuary, to see Your power and Your glory.

Because Your lovingkindness is better than life, my lips shall praise You. Thus I will bless You while I live;I will lift up my hands in Your name...And my mouth shall praise You with joyful lips...I meditate on You in the night watches.

Because You have been my help, therefore in the shadow of Your wings I will rejoice. My soul follows close behind You; Your right hand upholds me. Psalm 63:1-3,4,5,6,7-8 - NIV

_____
_____
_____
_____
_____
_____
_____

Sunday

Seeking with faith, hope, and love pleases our Lord and finding Him pleases the soul, filling it full of joy. And so I learned that as long as God allows us to struggle on this earth, seeking is as good as seeing.

— JULIAN OF NORWICH, 13TH CENTURY

Prayer

Dear Lord, I so long in my heart to know You deeply, intimately, personally. I know You created me with a void that can only be filled with You. I love to be in Your presence where peace and incredible joy fill my heart. Help me, Lord, to see this day as another opportunity for me to commune with You, that I will take time to seek to know you more, to rest and abide in Your presence. In Jesus Name, Amen.

∼

*J*ournaling Your Journey *Spiritual insights - Conversations with God - Favorite verses - Prayers - Struggles, Joys...*

_____
_____
_____
_____
_____
_____
_____
_____
_____
_____
_____
_____
_____
_____
_____
_____

This Week's Gratitude - Praise - Thanksgiving

_____
_____
_____
_____
_____

_____
_____
_____
_____
_____
_____
_____
_____
_____
_____
_____

✝✝✝

WEEK 41 – YOUR NEW NAME, HIS SEAL

And you will be called by a new name. You will also be a crown of beauty in the hand of the Lord. Isa 62:2-3

Monday

You shall also make a plate of pure gold and shall engrave on it, like the engravings of a seal, 'Holy to the Lord.' You shall fasten it on a blue cord, and it shall be on the turban; it shall be at the front of the turban. It shall be on Aaron's forehead. Exodus 28:36-38 - NAS

———

you also… are being built up as a spiritual house for a holy priesthood, to offer up spiritual sacrifices acceptable to God through Jesus Christ. 1 Peter 2:5 - NAS

———

His name will be on their foreheads.
Revelation 22:4 - NIV

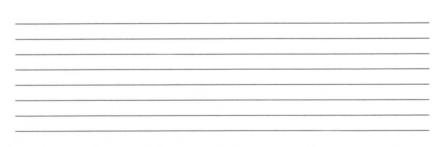

Tuesday

In Him you also trusted, after you heard the word of truth, the gospel of your salvation; in whom also, having believed, you were sealed with the Holy Spirit of promise. Ephesians 1:13, 14 - NKJ

_____

_____

_____

_____

_____

_____

_____

_____

~

Wednesday

Now it is God who makes both us and you stand firm in Christ. He anointed us, set his seal of ownership on us, and put his Spirit in our hearts as a deposit, guaranteeing what is to come. 2 Corinthians 1:21, 22 - NIV

_____

_____

_____

_____

_____

_____

_____

~

Thursday

Nevertheless, the firm foundation of God stands, having this seal, the Lord knows those who are His, and, Everyone who names the name of the Lord is to abstain from wickedness. — Let us rejoice and be glad and give the glory to Him, for the marriage of the Lamb has come and His bride has made herself ready. It was given to her to clothe herself in fine linen, bright and clean; for the fine linen is the righteous acts of the saints.. . . "Blessed are those who are invited to the marriage supper of the Lamb." And he said to me, "These are true words of God." 2 Timothy 2:19; Revelation 19:7-9

_____

_____

_____

Friday

*I will write on him the name of my God and the name of the city of my God,
the new Jerusalem, which is coming down out of heaven from my God; and I
will also write on him my new name. Revelation 3:12 - NIV*

~

Saturday

*The LORD is good, A stronghold in the day of trouble, And He knows those
who take refuge in Him. - I am the good shepherd, and know my sheep.
Nahum 1:7; John 10:14 - NAS*

~

Sunday

Prayer

*Oh Lord, by Who's grace I live and move an have my being, guide me through
the hours of this week. Teach me to be thoughtful toward those I meet, and,
above all to love! Open my understanding that I may find joy and delight in
Your Word, which alone can sanctify the heart and mind. I thank You for our
daily bread and every blessing that has come into our home. Watch over us
and protect us and keep us steadfast in faith. In Jesus glorious name, Amen.*

~

Journaling Your Journey *Spiritual insights - Conversations with God - Favorite verses - Prayers - Struggles, Joys...*

_____

_____

_____

_____

_____

_____

_____

_____

_____

_____

_____

_____

_____

_____

_____

_____

_____

This Week's Gratitude - Praise - Thanksgiving

_____

_____

_____

_____

_____

_____

_____

_____

_____

_____

_____

_____

_____

_____

✝✝✝

WEEK 42 – HE IS ABLE

Trust in the Lord with all your heart ... Proverbs 3:5

Monday
Able to do exceeding abundantly above all that we ask or think.
Ephesians 3:20 - KJV

~

Tuesday
He is able to save forever those who draw near to God through Him, since He
always lives to make intercession for them. Hebrews 7:25 - NAS

Wednesday

Able to make all grace abound to you, that always having all sufficiency in everything, you may have an abundance for every good deed;
2 Corinthians 9:8 - NAS

_____
_____
_____
_____
_____
_____
_____
_____
_____

≈

Thursday

"Do you believe that I am able to do this?" "Yes, Lord," they replied. . .
"According to your faith will it be done to you." Matthew 9:28, 29 - NIV

_____
_____
_____
_____
_____
_____
_____
_____

≈

Friday

For our citizenship is in heaven, from which also we eagerly wait for a Savior, the Lord Jesus Christ;who will transform our lowly body that it may be conformed to His glorious body, according to the working by which He is able even to subdue all things to Himself. Philippians 3:20, 21 - NKJ

_____
_____
_____
_____
_____
_____
_____
_____

Saturday

- *Able to aid those who are tempted. Hebrews 2:18 - NKJ*
- *Able to guard what I have entrusted to Him until that day. 2 Timothy 1:12 - NAS*
- *Able to keep you from stumbling, and to make you stand in the presence of His glory blameless with great joy. Jude 1:24 - NAS*

_____
_____
_____
_____
_____
_____
_____
_____

Sunday

The Two Listeners

Remember that life's difficulties and troubles are not intended to arrest your progress, but to increase your speed. Whatever it is must be surmounted, overcome. Remember this. It is as a race. Nothing must daunt you.

Do not let a difficulty conquer you. My strength will be there awaiting you. Nothing is too small to be faced and overcome if you are abiding with Me. Rise to conquer. It is the path of victory I would have you tread. There can be no failure with Me.

"Now unto Him that is able to keep you from falling, and to present you faultless before the presence of His glory with exceeding Joy ..." - KJV

∿

Journaling Your Journey Spiritual insights - Conversations with God - Favorite verses - Prayers - Struggles, Joys...

_____
_____
_____
_____
_____
_____
_____
_____
_____

_____
_____
_____
_____
_____
_____
_____
_____

This Week's Gratitude - Praise - Thanksgiving

_____
_____
_____
_____
_____
_____
_____
_____
_____
_____
_____
_____
_____
_____

✝✝✝

WEEK 43 - FRUIT OF MEEKNESS

There is Great Strength in a Gentle Quiet Spirit

Monday
The fruit of the Spirit is ... meekness.
Galatians 5:22, 23

"Blessed are the poor in spirit, for theirs is the kingdom of heaven."
"Blessed are the gentle, for they shall inherit the earth."
Matthew 5:3,5

_____
_____
_____
_____
_____
_____
_____
_____
_____

~

Tuesday
...the unfading beauty of a gentle and quiet spirit,
which is of great worth in God's sight.
1 Peter 3:4 - NIV

_____
_____
_____

_____

_____

_____

_____

_____

_____

~

Wednesday

*... "I assure you and most solemnly say to you, unless you repent
[that is, change your inner self—your old way of thinking,
live changed lives] and become like children [trusting, humble,
and forgiving], you will never enter the kingdom of heaven.*

*Therefore, whoever humbles himself like this child
is greatest in the kingdom of heaven. Whoever receives and welcomes
one child like this in My name receives Me.*
Matthew 18:3,4-5 - AMP

_____

_____

_____

_____

_____

_____

_____

_____

~

Thursday

*Take My yoke upon you and learn from Me, for I am gentle and
humble in heart, and you will find rest for your souls. For My yoke is
easy and My burden is light. Matthew 11:29-30 - NAS*

_____

_____

_____

_____

_____

_____

~

Friday

He was oppressed, and he was afflicted, yet he opened not his mouth: he is brought as a lamb to the slaughter, and as a sheep before her shearers is dumb, so he openeth not his mouth. Isaiah 53:7 - KJV

∾

Saturday

The meek ... shall increase their joy in the LORD, and the poor among men shall rejoice in the Holy One of Israel. Isaiah 29:19 - KJV

∾

Sunday

Meekness is the absence of judgment:

"If you judge people you have no time to love them."

— MOTHER TERESA

Prayer

Dear God, I come humbly before You asking that You place in me a gentle heart of meekness — That As my Savior I would not break even a small bruised blade of grass. Help me to see others as You do, not judging by appearance but with an eternal perspective, seeing them with compassion for whatever the circumstances. To view them as a lamb that has gone astray desperately needing help.

Increase my faith and love within me so I am always ready to dry the tears of those who weep, to strengthen those who are feeble, so that that they may come to know Your love, Your redemption, and Your friendship. In Jesus Name. Amen

~

*J***ournaling Your Journey** *Spiritual insights - Conversations with God - Favorite verses - Prayers - Struggles, Joys...*

_____
_____
_____
_____
_____
_____
_____
_____
_____
_____
_____
_____
_____
_____

This Week's Gratitude - Praise - Thanksgiving

_____
_____
_____
_____
_____
_____
_____
_____
_____
_____
_____
_____
_____

✝✝✝

WEEK 44 - KINDNESS

So, as those who have been chosen of God, holy and beloved, put on a heart of compassion, kindness, humility, gentleness and patience.
Colossians 3:12

Monday

Behold, My Servant, whom I uphold; My chosen one in whom My soul delights. . . He will not cry out or raise His voice, Nor make His voice heard in the street. A bruised reed He will not break, And a dimly burning wick He will not extinguish; He will faithfully bring forth justice. Isaiah 42:1-2 - NAS

_____

_____

_____

_____

_____

_____

_____

_____

~

Tuesday

. . . in order that in the coming ages he might show the incomparable riches of his grace, expressed in his kindness to us in Christ Jesus. For it is by grace you have been saved, through faith-- and this not from yourselves, it is the gift of God. Ephesians 2:7-8 - NIV

_____

_____

_____

_____

_____
_____
_____
_____
_____

~

Wednesday
The fruit of the spirit is . .. kindness.
—What is desirable in a man is his kindness. . .
She opens her mouth in wisdom,
And the teaching of kindness is on her tongue.
Galatians 5:22; Proverbs 19:22; 31:26 - NAS

_____
_____
_____
_____
_____
_____
_____

~

Thursday
Do not let kindness and truth leave you;
Bind them around your neck,
Write them on the tablet of your heart.
So you will find favor and good repute
In the sight of God and man.
Proverbs 3:3-4 - NAS

_____
_____
_____
_____
_____
_____

~

Friday

How priceless is your unfailing love, O God!
People take refuge in the shadow of your wings.

They feast on the abundance of your house;
you give them drink from your river of delights.

For with you is the fountain of life;
in your light we see light. Psalm 36:7-9 - NIV

~

Saturday

But when the goodness and loving kindness
of God our Savior appeared,
He saved us, not because of works
done by us in righteousness,
but according to his own mercy,
by the washing of regeneration and
renewal of the Holy Spirit,

. . . so that being justified by his grace
we might become heirs
according to the hope of eternal life.
Titus 3:4-5,7 - ESV

~

Sunday

Constant kindness can accomplish much. As the sun makes ice melt, kindness causes misunderstanding, mistrust, and hostility to evaporate.

— ALBERT SCHWEITZER

Prayer

O Great God, You are merciful and gracious, patient, and abundant in goodness and truth, I have experienced in many ways Your never-failing fatherly care and safely reached the end of another week. With thanksgiving I exalt You as the source of many blessings that have come upon me. Graciously protect me from accidents and every form of sin and evil in the coming week, and I ask that You bless the work of my hands as if all my efforts are done unto You. Teach me to see ever more clearly that life and happiness, health and daily bread, and peace of heart, forgiveness of sins, and the home in heaven are gifts of Your divine grace. With all my heart I desire that my every thought and action may be a testimony of You living in my heart and guiding my life every moment, that others may come to know You and Your loving kindness through me. In Jesus Name. Amen

ournaling Your Journey Spiritual insights - Conversations with God - Favorite verses - Prayers - Struggles, Joys...

_____

_____

_____

_____

_____

_____

_____

_____

_____

_____

_____

_____

_____

_____

_____

_____

_____

_____

This Week's Gratitude - Praise - Thanksgiving

✝✝✝

WEEK 45 - PRAISE

Speaking to one another in psalms and hymns and spiritual songs,
singing and making melody with your heart to the Lord. Eph 5:19

Monday
Reasons to praise Him:

Having been reconciled, we shall be saved by His life!
For in Him all the fulness of Deity dwells in bodily form,
and in Him you have been made complete.
Romans 5:10; Colossians 2:9, 10 - NAS

Awaiting and confidently expecting the [fulfillment of our]
blessed hope and the glorious appearing of our great
God and Savior, Christ Jesus, who [willingly] gave Himself
[to be crucified] on our behalf to redeem us and
purchase our freedom from all wickedness,
and to purify for Himself a chosen and very special people
to be His own possession, who are enthusiastic for doing what is good.
Titus 2:13, 14 - AMP

_____

_____

_____

_____

_____

_____

_____

_____

_____

∾

Tuesday

Blessed and worthy of praise be the God and Father of our Lord Jesus Christ, who has blessed us with every spiritual blessing in the heavenly realms in Christ, just as [in His love] He chose us in Christ [actually selected us for Himself as His own] before the foundation of the world, so that we would be holy [that is, consecrated, set apart for Him, purpose-driven] and blameless in His sight. Ephesians 1:3-4 - AMP

_____

_____

_____

_____

_____

_____

_____

_____

❧

Wednesday
*Praise be to the God and Father of our Lord Jesus Christ!
In his great mercy he has given us new birth into a living hope through the resurrection of Jesus Christ from the dead, and into an inheritance that can never perish, spoil or fade-- kept in heaven for you.
1 Peter 1:3-4 - NIV*

_____

_____

_____

_____

_____

_____

_____

_____

❧

Thursday
*Shout joyfully to the Lord, all the earth.
Serve the Lord with gladness;
Come before Him with joyful singing.*

*Know that the Lord Himself is God;
It is He who has made us, and not we ourselves;
We are His people and the sheep of His pasture.*

Enter His gates with thanksgiving
And His courts with praise.
Give thanks to Him, bless His name.

For the Lord is good;
His lovingkindness is everlasting
And His faithfulness to all generations.
Psalm 100 - NAS

~

Friday

Oh give thanks to the Lord, call upon His name;
Make known His deeds among the peoples.
Sing to Him, sing praises to Him; Speak of all His wonders.
Glory in His holy name; Let the heart of those who seek the Lord be glad.
Seek the Lord and His strength; Seek His face continually.
Remember His wonders which He has done,
His marvels and the judgments uttered by His mouth...
He is the Lord our God; His judgments are in all the earth.
Psalm 105: 1-5, 7 - NAS

~

Saturday

I will give You thanks with all my heart; I will sing praises to You before the gods. I will bow down toward Your holy temple and give thanks to Your name for Your lovingkindness and Your truth; For You have magnified Your word according to all Your name.

Psalm 138 - NAS

_____
_____
_____
_____
_____
_____
_____
_____

≈

Sunday

Prayer

Heavenly Father, I desire to praise You with my whole heart! That Your glory may be seen in me, as a tribute to Your great eternal love and blessings. Please provide health and strength, courage and confidence, as the tasks of another week come before me. Graciously protect me from accidents and every from of sin and evil, and bless the work of my hands. Please make me mindful that I am but a stranger and pilgrim in this present world. Let me not devote my efforts this week to purposes unworthy of You. This life is passing away, help me focus on Your eternal work and plan in all love and peace. In Jesus Name, Amen.

≈

J **ournaling Your Journey** *Spiritual insights - Conversations with God - Favorite verses - Prayers - Struggles, Joys...*

_____
_____
_____
_____
_____
_____
_____
_____
_____
_____

_____
_____
_____
_____
_____
_____

This Week's Gratitude - Praise - Thanksgiving

_____
_____
_____
_____
_____
_____
_____
_____
_____
_____
_____
_____
_____

✝✝✝

WEEK 46 – FRUIT OF FAITH

We walk by faith, not by sight. 2 Corinthians 5:7

Monday
I have been crucified with Christ and I no longer live, but Christ lives in me. The life I live in the body, I live by faith in the Son of God, who loved me and gave himself for me. Galatians 2:20 - NIV

~

Tuesday
Therefore, having been justified by faith, we have peace with God through our Lord Jesus Christ, through whom also we have obtained our introduction by faith into this grace in which we stand; and we exult in hope of the glory of God. Romans 5:1-2 - NAS

_____
_____
_____
_____

~

Wednesday
For we through the Spirit, by faith, are waiting for the hope of righteousness.
. . . faith working through love. Galatians 5:5,6 - NAS

_____
_____
_____
_____
_____
_____

~

Thursday
Though you have not seen him, you love him;
and even though you do not see him now,
you believe in him and are filled
with an inexpressible and glorious joy,
for you are receiving the goal of your faith,
the salvation of your souls.
1 Peter 1:8, 9 - NIV

_____
_____
_____
_____
_____
_____

~

Friday
You believe that there is one God, you do well. Even the demons believe
—and tremble! But do you want to know, O foolish man, that faith
without works is dead. James 2:19-20 - NKJ

_____
_____
_____
_____
_____
_____
_____
_____

Saturday

The Peril of Unbelief

Take care, brethren, that there not be in any one of you an evil, unbelieving heart that falls away from the living God. But encourage one another day after day, as long as it is still called 'Today,' so that none of you will be hardened by the deceitfulness of sin. — I do believe; help me overcome my unbelief! Hebrews 3:12-13; Mark 9:24 - NAS

_____
_____
_____
_____
_____
_____
_____

∽

Sunday

Oh, for a faith that will not shrink
Tho' pressed by many a foe;
That will not tremble on the brink
Of poverty or woe.

A faith that shines more bright and clear
When tempests rage without
That, when in danger, know no fear,
In darkness feels no doubt.

A faith that keeps the narrow way
Till life's last spark is fled
And with a pure and heavenly ray
Lights up the dying bed.

William H. Bathurst, 1831

~

*J*ournaling *Your Journey* *Spiritual insights - Conversations with God -*
Favorite verses - Prayers - Struggles, Joys...

_____
_____
_____
_____
_____
_____
_____
_____
_____
_____
_____
_____
_____
_____
_____
_____
_____
_____

This Week's Gratitude - Praise - Thanksgiving

_____
_____
_____
_____
_____
_____
_____
_____
_____
_____
_____
_____

✝✝✝

WEEK 47 – THANKFUL FOR CHRIST OUR SAVIOR

I am the Living One; I was dead, and behold I am alive for ever and ever! Revelation 1:18

Monday

And high above on the throne was a figure like that of a man. For there is one God and one mediator between God and men, the man Christ Jesus, Ezekiel 1:26; 1 Timothy 2:5 - NIV

_____
_____
_____
_____
_____
_____
_____
_____

~

Tuesday

For in Christ all the fullness of the Deity lives in bodily form, and you have been given fullness in Christ, who is the head over every power and authority. Colossians 2:9-10 - NIV

_____
_____
_____
_____
_____

_____

_____

~

Wednesday

For though He was crucified in weakness, yet He lives by the power of God. For we also are weak in Him, but we shall live with Him by the power of God . 2 Corinthians 13:4 - NKJ

_____
_____
_____
_____
_____
_____
_____
_____

~

Thursday

Forasmuch ... as the children are partakers of flesh and blood, he also himself likewise took part of the same; that through death he might destroy him that had the power of death. Hebrews 2:14 - KJV

_____
_____
_____
_____
_____
_____
_____
_____

~

Friday

Behold, My Servant, whom I uphold;
My chosen one in whom My soul delights.
I have put My Spirit upon Him;
He will bring forth justice to the nations.
He will not cry out or raise His voice,
Nor make His voice heard in the street.

A bruised reed He will not break

And a dimly burning wick He will not extinguish;
He will faithfully bring forth justice.
He will not be disheartened or crushed
Until He has established justice in the earth;
And the coastlands will wait expectantly for His law.

Thus says God the Lord,
Who created the heavens and stretched them out,
Who spread out the earth and its offspring,
Who gives breath to the people on it
And spirit to those who walk in it,

I am the Lord, I have called You in righteousness,
I will also hold You by the hand and watch over You,
And I will appoint You as a covenant to the people,
As a light to the nations, To open blind eyes,
To bring out prisoners from the dungeon
And those who dwell in darkness from the prison.
Isaiah 42:1-7 - NAS

_____
_____
_____
_____
_____
_____
_____
_____
_____

∾

Saturday

Christ, having been raised from the dead, is never to die again; death
no longer is master over Him. For the death that He died, He died to
sin, once for all; but the life that He lives, He lives to God.
Romans 6:9, 10 - NAS

_____
_____
_____
_____
_____
_____
_____
_____
_____

Sunday

Thanksgiving Prayer:

Great and merciful God and Father, after who the whole family in heaven and earth is named, I appear before You with gratitude in my heart and praise on my lips. I am so very grateful for Your gift of eternal life through Jesus. I extol You Who has opened Your hands to supply our needs and Your heart to invite us into relationship with You!

Thank You for the extreme joy and peace we can only find You alone. Help me to ever come closer to You, to be increasingly aware of Your presence with me moment by moment. Kindle in me a greater love that I may serve You and those around me. In Jesus Name, Amen.

～

Journaling Your Journey Spiritual insights - Conversations with God - Favorite verses - Prayers - Struggles, Joys...

_____
_____
_____
_____
_____
_____
_____
_____
_____
_____
_____
_____
_____
_____
_____
_____

This Week's Gratitude - Praise - Thanksgiving

_____
_____
_____
_____
_____
_____

✝✝✝

WEEK 48 – REJOICE IN HOPE!

Rejoice in the Lord always: and again I say, Rejoice. Philippians 4:4

Monday

I will rejoice greatly in the Lord,
My soul will exult in my God;
For He has clothed me with garments of salvation,
He has wrapped me with a robe of righteousness,
As a bridegroom decks himself with a garland,
And as a bride adorns herself with her jewels.
For as a young man marries a virgin, …
And as the bridegroom rejoices over the bride,
So your God will rejoice over you.
Isaiah 61:10: 62:5 - NAS

Tuesday

May the God of hope fill you with all joy and peace as you trust in him, so that you may overflow with hope by the power of the Holy Spirit. Romans 15:13 - NIV

≈

Wednesday

through whom we have gained access by faith into this grace in which we now stand. And we rejoice in the hope of the glory of God. Romans 5:2 - NIV

≈

Thursday

Though you have not seen him, you love him; and even though you do not see him now, you believe in him and are filled with an inexpressible and glorious joy. 1 Peter 1:8 - NIV

Friday
Praise be to the God and Father of our Lord Jesus Christ! In his great mercy he has given us new birth into a living hope through the resurrection of Jesus Christ from the dead, and into an inheritance that can never perish, spoil or fade-- kept in heaven for you.
1 Peter 1:3-4 - NIV

_____
_____
_____
_____
_____
_____
_____
_____

~

Saturday
. . . Rejoicing in hope. —
faith and love that spring from the hope stored up for you in heaven and about which you have already heard in the true message of the gospel. Romans 12:1 - KJV; Colossians 1:5 - NIV

_____
_____
_____
_____
_____
_____
_____

~

Sunday

The Two Listeners
Your Hope is in the Lord. More and more set your hopes on Me... Do not try to find answers to the mysteries of the world. Learn to know Me more and more, and in that knowledge you will have all the answers you need here. Joy in Me, trust in Me, share all of Life with Me. . . And give Me the joy of sharing everything with you!

*J**ournaling Your Journey** Spiritual insights - Conversations with God - Favorite verses - Prayers - Struggles, Joys...*

_____

This Week's Gratitude - Praise - Thanksgiving

_____

✝✝✝

WEEK 49 – COMPASSION OF GOD

The LORD's lovingkindnesses indeed never cease, For His compassions never fail. They are new every morning; Lam 3:22, 23

Monday
Like an eagle that stirs up its nest and hovers over its young, that spreads its wings to catch them and carries them on its pinions. The LORD alone led him; no foreign god was with him. Deuteronomy 32:11, 12 - NIV

_____
_____
_____
_____
_____
_____
_____
_____

~

Tuesday
He saw a great multitude, and felt compassion for them, and healed their sick. Matthew 14:14 - NAS

_____
_____
_____
_____
_____
_____
_____

<u>Wednesday</u>
Bless the Lord, O my soul,
And all that is within me, bless His holy name.
Bless the Lord, O my soul,
And forget none of His benefits;

Who redeems your life from the pit,
Who crowns you with lovingkindness and compassion;
Who satisfies your years with good things,
So that your youth is renewed like the eagle.

The Lord is compassionate and gracious,
Slow to anger and abounding in lovingkindness.
Psalm 103:1-2,4-5,8 - NAS

_____
_____
_____
_____
_____
_____
_____
_____
_____

∼

<u>Thursday</u>
Are not two sparrows sold for a penny?
Yet not one of them will fall to the ground
apart from the will of your Father.
And even the very hairs of your head
are all numbered. Matthew 10:29-30 - NIV

_____
_____
_____
_____
_____
_____
_____
_____

∼

Friday
The Lord is full of compassion and mercy.
James 5:11 - NIV

―――――――――――――――――――――――――――
―――――――――――――――――――――――――――
―――――――――――――――――――――――――――
―――――――――――――――――――――――――――
―――――――――――――――――――――――――――
―――――――――――――――――――――――――――
―――――――――――――――――――――――――――
―――――――――――――――――――――――――――

≈

Saturday
As a father has compassion on his children, so the LORD has compassion on those who fear him; - Jesus Christ is the same yesterday and today and forever.
Psalm 103:13; Hebrews 13:8 - NIV

―――――――――――――――――――――――――――
―――――――――――――――――――――――――――
―――――――――――――――――――――――――――
―――――――――――――――――――――――――――
―――――――――――――――――――――――――――
―――――――――――――――――――――――――――
―――――――――――――――――――――――――――
―――――――――――――――――――――――――――

≈

Sunday

The Gospel shows the Father's grace,
Who sent His Son to save our race,
Proclaims how Jesus lived and died
That man might thus be justified.

It sets the Lamb before our eyes,
Who made th'atoning sacrifice,
And calls the souls with guilt opprest
To come and find eternal rest.

Matthias Loy, 1863

≈

*J*ournaling *Your Journey* *Spiritual insights - Conversations with God -*
Favorite verses - Prayers - Struggles, Joys...

_____
_____
_____
_____
_____
_____
_____
_____
_____
_____
_____
_____
_____
_____
_____

This Week's Gratitude - Praise - Thanksgiving

_____
_____
_____
_____
_____
_____
_____
_____
_____
_____
_____
_____
_____
_____
_____

✝✝✝

WEEK 50 – GOD'S THOUGHTS TOWARD US

... I am poor and needy; Yet the LORD thinks upon me. Ps 40:17 - NKJ

Monday
Many, O LORD my God, are Your wonderful works Which You have done;
And Your thoughts toward us Cannot be recounted to You in order; ... They are
more than can be numbered. Psalm 40:5 - NKJ

_____
_____
_____
_____
_____
_____
_____
_____

~

Tuesday
For I know the thoughts that I think toward you, says the LORD, thoughts of
peace and not of evil, to give you a future and a hope. Jeremiah 29:11 - NKJ

_____
_____
_____
_____
_____
_____
_____

Wednesday
How precious also are Your thoughts to me, O God! How great is the sum of them! If I should count them, they would be more in number than the sand; When I awake, I am still with You. Psalm 139:17, 18 - NKJ

~

Thursday
"For My thoughts are not your thoughts, Nor are your ways My ways," says the LORD. "For as the heavens are higher than the earth, So are My ways higher than your ways, And My thoughts than your thoughts." Isaiah 55:8, 9 - NKJ

~

Friday
The Lord is not slow about His promise, as some count slowness, but is patient toward you, not wishing for any to perish but for all to come to repentance. 2 Peter 3:9 - NAS

Saturday

I love the Lord, because He hears
My voice and my supplications.
Because He has inclined His ear to me,
Therefore I shall call upon Him as long as I live.

The cords of death encompassed me
And the terrors of Sheol came upon me;
I found distress and sorrow.
Then I called upon the name of the Lord:
"O Lord, I beseech You, save my life!"

Gracious is the Lord, and righteous;
Yes, our God is compassionate.
Psalm 116:1-5 - NAS

Sunday

Prayer

Heavenly Father, I am so very thankful that You have blessed me with the
ability to feel Your loving compassion toward me personally! And so I am filled
with joy and peace. And it gives me confidence to walk through this week
knowing I am not alone. Help me to become ever more aware of Your loving
presence through every minute of each day, so that my joy may be complete in
You! In Jesus Name, Amen.

Journaling Your Journey Spiritual insights - Conversations
with God - Favorite verses - Prayers - Struggles, Joys...

This Week's Gratitude - Praise - Thanksgiving

✝✝✝

WEEK 51 – GOD IS CHANGELESS

From everlasting to everlasting You are God. Psalm 90:2

Monday
*But you remain the same, and your years will never end. The Mighty God,
Everlasting Father, Prince of Peace. Psalm 102:27; Isaiah 9:6 - NIV*

_____

_____

_____

_____

_____

_____

_____

_____

~

Tuesday
*Before the mountains were born or you brought forth the earth and the world,
from everlasting to everlasting you are God. Psalm 90:2 - NIV*

_____

_____

_____

_____

_____

_____

_____

_____

Wednesday

Every good and perfect gift is from above, coming down from the Father of the heavenly lights, who does not change like shifting shadows. James 1:17 - NIV

~

Thursday

Jesus Christ is the same yesterday and today, yes and forever. - Do not be afraid; I am the first and the last, Hebrews 13:8; Revelation 1:17 - NAS

~

Friday

But because Jesus lives forever, he has a permanent priesthood. Therefore he is able to save completely those who come to God through him, because he always lives to intercede for them. Such a high priest meets our need-- one who is holy, blameless, pure, set apart from sinners, exalted above the heavens.
Hebrews 7:24-25 - NIV

Saturday

Of old You founded the earth,
And the heavens are the work of Your hands.
Even they will perish, but You endure;
And all of them will wear out like a garment;
Like clothing You will change them and they will be changed.
But You are the same, and Your years will not come to an end.
Psalm 102:25-27 - NAS

_____
_____
_____
_____
_____
_____
_____
_____

∾

Sunday

Prayer

O Great God, You are merciful and gracious, patient, and abundant in
goodness and truth. Thankful again, I have experienced in many ways Your
never-failing fatherly care and safely reached the end of another week. Grant
me help from above that I may prove to be salt and light to all those around
me, and fearlessly confess my faith in Jesus Christ, my Redeemer. Give me
strength to resist more earnestly the allurements of anything that distracts me
from that pure relationship with You, which fills me with joy and peace
abundantly. This I ask in the name of my Lord Jesus Christ. Amen.

∾

*J***ournaling Your Journey** *Spiritual insights - Conversations with God -*
Favorite verses - Prayers - Struggles, Joys...

_____
_____
_____
_____
_____
_____
_____
_____

This Week's Gratitude - Praise - Thanksgiving

✝✝✝

WEEK 52 * CHRISTMAS WEEK *

THE LONG AWAITED MESSIAH HAS COME – Redeemer of Mankind!

Monday

For unto us a Child is born, Unto us a Son is given; And the government will be upon His shoulder. And His name will be called Wonderful, Counselor, Mighty God, Everlasting Father, Prince of Peace. Isaiah 9:6 - NKJ

_____
_____
_____
_____
_____
_____
_____
_____

~

Tuesday

God was manifest in the flesh. The kindness and love of God our Savior toward man appeared. 1 Timothy 3:16; Titus 3:4 - KJV

_____
_____
_____
_____
_____
_____
_____

Wednesday

But when the time had fully come, God sent his Son, born of a woman, born under law, to redeem those under law, that we might receive the full rights of sons. Galatians 4:4, 5 - NIV

_____

_____

_____

_____

_____

_____

_____

_____

∾

Thursday

Emmanuel, . . . God with us.-- The Word was made flesh, and dwelt among us, (and we beheld his glory, the glory as of the only begotten of the Father), full of grace and truth.
Matthew 1:23; John 1:14 - KJV

_____

_____

_____

_____

_____

_____

_____

∾

Friday

God . . .in these last days has spoken to us in His Son, whom He appointed heir of all things, Hebrews 1:1,2 - NAS

_____

_____

_____

_____

_____

_____

_____

_____

Saturday

In this was manifested the love of God toward us, because that God sent his only begotten Son into the world, that we might live through him. Herein is love, not that we loved God, but that he loved us, and sent his Son to be the propitiation for our sins. 1 John 4:9, 10 - KJV

~

Sunday

Christmas Prayer:

Jesus, my Savior, as I stand in spirit at Your lowly manger, I bow my knees in reverent worship of that great mystery revealed in Your birth in Bethlehem's stable. Here lies God manifest in the flesh.

O Jesus, teach me humbly to believe what reason cannot comprehend, and with childlike faith, to accept this mystery that no created mind can fully understand. At Your humble resting place, my Redeemer, I joyfully praise Your love and grace. You left Your Father's throne – for me. You have taken the sins of the world upon Yourself – for me. You are willing to fulfill all righteousness – for me.

Savior, I thank You for Your unspeakable love, and I pray, let me ever be faithful to You. As Your love has drawn You from heaven to earth, so let Your love draw me from earth to heaven to be Yours in time and eternity. Amen.

~

Journaling Your Journey Spiritual insights - Conversations with God - Favorite verses - Prayers - Struggles, Joys...

This Week's Gratitude - Praise - Thanksgiving

✝✝✝

MAY GOD BLESS YOUR SPIRITUAL JOURNEY

PRAYER OF BLESSING FOR YOU

PRAYER FOR YOU - BELOVED IN CHRIST

May our Lord and Shepherd keep you safe in the pastures of His loving care. May He feed you with the heavenly food that provides growth and strength. And surround You with His presence as you tread in places of trouble.

We will meet some day in that lovely place where the Sun of Light shines evermore. Until then, may He continually shine His face upon you and keep you in peace.

In the Name of our Great Savior, Jesus Christ
Amen

ANCIENT IRISH BLESSINGS

May God give you...
For every storm, a rainbow,
For every tear, a smile,

For every care, a promise,
And a blessing in each trial.
For every problem life sends,
A faithful friend to share,
For every sigh, a sweet song,
And an answer for each prayer.

God Bless You Eternally

Providing books with solid Scriptural foundation, to feed Jesus' sheep and lambs, is our mission at Kingdom Life Books & Kingdom Life 365.

Serving us full time, Lee Kowal's credentials begin with years of formal training and a Masters of Divinity from Moody Seminary, graduating with High Honors. After a 33-year career in Engineering, Lee has now retired with a single desire, to serve God in His mission on earth.

Our high view of Scripture and Faith in Him lead us to treat every word placed in print as ministry unto the Lord -- Scripture is presented with utmost respect, diligence, and care.

If this devotional has blessed you, we humbly ask that you consider leaving a review at online site where purchased. Reviews help us to continue this ministry. Thank You.

✝ ✝ ✝

Made in the USA
San Bernardino, CA
14 March 2019